THIS SIDE
OF NORMAL

Ten Year Testimony of Trials and Faith

By Kerrie M. Baker

ISBN: 978-1-7350715-0-3: This Side of Normal (paperback)

978-1-7350715-1-0: This Side of Normal (hardcover)

978-1-7350715-2-7: This Side of Normal (eBook)

Dedication

   I remember it so clearly, even though I was just a kid. I was unable to make it to church on Sunday morning. Strep throat again for the third time that year had me miserable. I was laying on the couch curled up in blankets when my parents walked into the living room. They were dressed for Sunday services. Mom with her hair curled and sprayed into perfect place, and my dad in golf style polo and nice black slacks. Bibles under their arms and car keys in hand they were ready to go. One look at me and the joy on their faces turned.

   After a moment of discussion, my dad kissed my mom and told her to go and enjoy service. He would stay home with me this time. I felt terrible. Not only in my body, but I couldn't help but feel like I was making my parents miss out on the joy they received from attending church. They both worked so hard during the week and taking care of us kids, they only time they socialized was before and after service. Here I was again, sick, and causing them to miss out on everything that going to church meant. They needed that time to worship God and learn more about Jesus, serve wherever they could, and see friends they hadn't spoken to in a week. They never said anything. As parents do, they just handled the situation.

It had only been about ten minutes after mom had left when my dad came from the kitchen. In his hand was a tray with a couple of crackers and two tiny cups of grape juice. There in our family home, my dad preached me the word of God for the first time. It was my first communion since I had been baptized. As he read the scriptures and we broke the bread and drank the juice, his eyes welled up with emotion. He told me then, quoting the Word of God, that I should always remember, where two or more are gathered, God is there; and since I carried Jesus in my heart, He counted as two or more. I would never be alone because God and Jesus were with me always.

So, I dedicate this to the one who set me on my path with Christ. To Gary W. Richardson. My father who always taught me that life is just life. It's okay to make a mistake, it's not about how you mess up, but how you deal with it later that matters. Most of all, you just gotta be Christ to people. Thank you for always believing in me Dad. I love and miss you, bunches.

1 Thessalonians 5:24

He who calls you is faithful, and He will do it.

Foreword

From the first time I met Kerrie at her business, I knew she was someone special in the Kingdom of God. She had all the qualities of a high-flying, anointed, woman of God without saying much—but every word she shared had power behind it. A story, a testimony and a lesson. After reading her book it has confirmed what I have known all along, that Kerrie embodied the Prophetic gift she has with class, charisma, and most importantly, genuineness. Today, as I write this foreword to her captivating memoir, I share words that I always hoped—and in many ways knew—I would have the chance to write. I highly recommend this book, the stories in it will change your life and confirm your gift! Kerrie, your gift will continue to change many lives as it has changed mine, thank you!!

Pastor JC Cantu

Table of Contents

Introduction

Thanks for purchasing This Side of Normal. I am excited to share a glimpse into a crazy hectic, never perfect, but perfectly wonderful life.

This book will take you through a ten-year period of my life. Every story is true. Every person is real. Every situation happened. Not all stories are for the faint of heart. This is my journey through heartache, health issues, pain, grief, trauma, demonic activity and much more.

Within these pages I want to show you how God is always faithful. He will never leave you or forsake you. Many of the stories you will read are just small pieces of a bigger puzzle. I am not someone that is extraordinary, or super important. I do not have a degree in theology, or in any other religious area. I am just a girl who loves her God, believes Jesus is His son who died for me (and you), and follows the guide of the Holy Spirit.

Don't wait another second to dive in. You will see how through all the craziness of life; God can work and move. No matter where you are in your walk with Christ, this book will show you that you can overcome anything! You may be living your best Christian life, or you may be just trying to survive from one day to the next. This book is for you.

Everyone has a story to tell. A testimony to share. This is part of mine. I pray that my story will give you hope. I pray that as you read this testimonial you will find that we all tend to live this side of normal.

Psalm 71:15-18 (NKJV)

[15] *My mouth shall tell of Your righteousness*
And Your salvation all the day,
For I do not know their limits.
[16] *I will go in the strength of the Lord God;*
I will make mention of Your righteousness, of Yours only.

[17] *O God, You have taught me from my youth;*
And to this day I declare Your wondrous works.
[18] *Now also when I am old and gray headed,*
O God, do not forsake me,
Until I declare Your strength to this generation,
Your power to everyone who is to come.

PART I: TRIALS

It was like it happened yesterday. Even all these years later I still remember every tiny detail of the day God used my prophetic gift. I was just a kid. I had just begun my seventh-grade year of school; I was twelve. My family had a doughnut shop. Dad made the doughnuts, my Grandmother ran the register, my Grandfather kept all the customers entertained, mom helped out when she wasn't teaching school, and my sister and I would go in the late evenings to clean. It was a family business in a small town, we all pitched in to make it work. Cleaning was by far my least favorite job, but someone had to do it. My sister was able to drive, so most of the time it was just her and I there late at night. We would wipe down all the tables, clean the display case, clean the windows, sweep and mop, disinfect the bathroom and so on. It wasn't a very big building. There were two entrances, the front door where customers would enter and the back where we would always come and go. The back door leads straight into the kitchen. There was a small bathroom at the back wall near the door on the right. The old white Formica tile covering the floor was chipped and worn. There was a large utility sink and cleaning station lining the right wall that wrapped around to a series of shelves that held all the ingredients for dad's baking. On the left side of the room was a large proofing oven, a deep fryer with wire racks to the right for cooling, a glazing station, and a final tray holding area. All of it stainless steel. In the very center of the room there was an enormous white topped table setting beside it was a mixing bowl at least two foot in diameter on a large frame about waist high. As you passed through the kitchen there was a small hallway with a door on the right that held the office. My grandmother had a large wooden desk with a glass top that was usually covered with bookkeeping stuff, papers and an ashtray full of cigarette buds. Her office chair was metal and green pleather on wheels and rolled pretty well over the hard-plastic floor covering below it. Beside the desk was another plain wooden chair that my dad would sit in and drink coffee for a break from being on his feet all night making breakfast for the town. Past the office, the hallway opened up into the dining and serving area. You could walk straight down the hall and behind the display case and cash register counter. The case was fairly large glass and stainless steel with three shelves slanted towards to front glass. On top were serving tissues and trays for the eat in customers and below were stacks of different boxes for those getting food to go. The register counter was tall enough that I had to use a step stool to reach the register when checking out customers. The other side of the room held four top tables with two sets pushed together so eight people could sit at once. There were six sets of tables all together, and many times they were completely full of townspeople. I learned all sorts of things listening to those customers and those memories are dear to me to this day.

As my sister and I started to the seven-mile drive to go clean the shop I started complaining that I didn't want to go. I didn't want to help her clean, I didn't care if she needed my help or not, I was just being a pain in the rear little sister. We argued to say the least and by the time we walked in the door my sister had decided I was done for. She even told me that if I did not start helping clean that she would call home and tell mom and dad how I was acting. That was enough to put the fear of God in me. I began helping her, but I had a sinking feeling deep in my gut. I had to call my best friend. I asked my sister if I could call Angi and of course she thought I was just making excuses not to do any cleaning. After the third time asking and hearing a lecture on my slacking I ran into the office and locked the door. My sister was furious. She was yelling at me through the door and I knew I would get in big trouble for not helping her, but my mind was made up. I picked up the phone and dialed Angi's number. It picked up on the third ring and before the person on the other end could say a word I began speaking. There was no caller ID back then, I was dialing her on a rotary phone for pity's sake. There was no way for her to know I was calling, or for her older brother or parents to know. More than that there was no way for me to know that I was even speaking to Angi and not one of the others whom she lived with. It was after all later than nine o'clock on a weekday, and we were twelve years old. But I started with "Hi, Angi. I am so very sorry your dad left. I am here if you need to talk." Deep sobs came from the receiver and I could hear Angi crying and asking me "How did you know? There's no way you could know. He literally just walked out of the door before the phone rang. My parents are getting a divorce." I could then hear her mom calling her in the background and Angi sputtered a quick "I'll call you later, I gotta go." The line fell silent. I don't really remember much after that except my sister continuing to yell at me for being lazy, and getting in big trouble for not helping, but where we made it home some two hours later, my mom and dad were still awake and I was sure I was going to get punished for "not helping my sister". Apparently, Angi's mom had called my parents and told them the whole story, even about me calling and was so thankful I had called. My mom and dad wanted to know why I had called her and said what I had said about Angi's dad, but I didn't have an answer for them. I didn't know myself. I didn't even know at the time that it was God stirring up my prophetic gifting to help my friend. I had no idea what a prophetic gift was. I had never even heard of such until much, much later in my life. But God used me completely in spite of me.

Angi was my closest childhood friend. We went everywhere together that our parents would allow, and honestly as we grew up, we ventured places they do not know about to this day. That, however, is a different story. I can even remember her and I making the decision, after attending church camp together, to be baptized at the same time. God had truly connected us, and even throughout the years, growing up, and moving apart, our Father really proved this connection over and over. Angi was an amazing friend. She knew I was different than most of the other friends we hung out with, but she would just laugh and say I was weird and that was it. She never pressed me for information, or ever acted like it was really a big deal. As young adults we connected again for a weekend Walk to Emmaus trip. Although much had happened in both our lives, it was like no time had passed on our friendship. To this day, I know hands down, if I ever needed to talk to someone, Angi would be there.

I always thought that the experience from our youth when her dad left, was for my benefit. With age comes some wisdom at least, and I honestly believe it was way more for her. After that any time I told her I had a bad feeling about something she never questioned it. For instance, if I told her I didn't think going to the movies was going to be a good idea, she would just say okay, let's just hang out here. Often enough, something crazy would happen at the movie theater, that we would have been in if we had gone. As the years progressed, God used me several times to connect with Angi. Once after we had graduated high school, she had called me to talk and before she got a chance to tell me, I blurted out "Oh my gosh, Angi, you're pregnant!" She laughed for a good while and said "Man, I can never surprise you, can I?"

The biggest event of God using me for my friend happened many years later from that night at the doughnut shop phone call. I was twenty-two, working as an EMT in a small town in central Texas. I was living far from a Godly life. I was definitely not who you would think God could use. He did however use me, like never before.

Working on the ambulance was a twenty-four-hour shift, so we had to sleep at the station. It wasn't uncommon for us to have very busy shifts and very slow shifts. I was on a slow shift for my first rotation, and that night I had the most horrible vivid dream I had ever had up to that time. I dreamt about Angi.

She was packing a lunch and getting things together to take to her husband who was working in another town about twenty miles away from their house. Her sister in law was helping her get all the food and goodies loaded into a little red car, and they were talking about what they were going to do with the kids after Angi got back from taking her husband lunch. She climbed in the car and waved goodbye to her sister in law and begins her trip in usual Angi fashion. That is, music up loud enough to hear over the window's down highway driving. I even saw her make the turn off the major highway to the little road headed to the small town when the engine light came on. Suddenly her car sputtered to a stop, but she managed to pull it to the side of the road. It wouldn't start. She got out of the car and popped open the hood. Shaking her head, she said "Guess the darn alternator finally gave out." Then a man in a dark colored truck pulled up behind her car. The sinking feeling in my gut was screaming as soon as I saw him. What came next was the only nightmare I wish I could have woken up from. He asked her to lean in and try to start the car again while he looked under the hood. Instead of going all the way to the front of the car he stood behind her, and with a fatal swoop as she leaned over into the car, he bashed her head in with a pipe. Knocked out instantly she was completely defenseless. One blow wasn't enough for this man. He hit her repeatedly and then raped her lifeless body.

I awoke violently tremoring and crying. Covered in sweat, I ran to our main office and picked up the phone. I had not talked to Angi in over five years. I didn't know her phone number. So, I prayed. "God, help me call my friend to warn her, please!" I began dialing a number and in two rings her mother answered. I frantically asked to speak to my friend and almost fainted when her mom told me she was out. I was so frightened I was too late. I knew I couldn't tell her mother everything I saw in my dream, that would be too much for her to handle. She told me she would have Angi call me the second she got back from the store. As I hung up, I began to fervently pray that God would take this burden off my friend. I even asked him to make it fall on me somehow, not to allow her to be murdered.

For about the longest five minutes of my life, I prayed. Then the phone rang. It was Angi. I told her I knew she was about to take lunch to her husband in another town, and I begged her to not go alone. I told her that I knew it would be bad, but I didn't want to tell her everything I had seen. I pleaded with her for quite a while until she told me that she had in fact been at the store to get the food for her husbands' lunch to take to him, and if she did not hurry, he would not be able to eat until much later tonight. She promised to take someone with her. In fact, her sister in law agreed to accompany her. She rushed to get off the phone but told me she would call when they had made it back home. After hanging up the phone, I prayed again for God to put the burden on me instead of her somehow. Then I sat down on the floor beside the desk and waited for her phone call. About six hours later she called and was laughing and told me that she knew I didn't have anything to worry about. Everything was fine and she was safe. At that point I told her what all I had seen in the dream. We cried together on the phone, and I thanked God she was okay.

The next morning when my full shift was over, I headed out to my car. It would not start. I tried everything. Nothing. It wouldn't even make that clicking sound as if it had a dead battery. This was a brand-new car. Had less than four hundred miles on it. Brand new. So, I called the dealership and they sent a mechanic to come take a look at it for me. For no reason the mechanic could find, the alternator was fried.

A month later, Angi and I sat together at a table for the Walk to Emmaus. We hugged, cried, and praised God for what He did that day, and what He did all those years before. That first call from the doughnut shop, that made my friend believe my bad feelings.

This was just the beginning of how God would, and still does, use me for His glory.

Romans 8:26 New King James Version (NKJV)

[26] Likewise the Spirit also helps in our weaknesses. For we do not know what we should pray for as we ought, but the Spirit Himself makes intercession for us with groanings which cannot be uttered.

Chapter One: Facing Death...and New Life

Hebrews 11:1 New Living Translation (NLT)

1 Faith shows the reality of what we hope for; it is the evidence of things we cannot see.

After the intense dream of my childhood friend, it was like my prophetic gifting had been stirred up to a roaring flame. Many times, I would tell my partners on the ambulance when we were about to go on a call and even what to expect when we arrived on scene. I had no idea though, that this was from God. I honestly believed something was wrong with me. Normal people were not able to do this. I just knew things. Like I said before, I was not living a Godly life. Not by any means. I was quite a horrible person. I was arrogant and very selfish. I did not care for my husband or children. I was living life for myself. I ended up a divorced, single mom of three. Then remarried because I did not know who I was or how to be okay with just being me. After divorcing my second husband I began to finally start seeing the person I was. I began working hard to raise my kids myself. I reconnected with family I had pushed away out of my own shame for many years. A friend from work invited me to church and we went often. I started dating a previous co-worker who I had been friends with for a few years, but I was not looking to be involved with anyone other than God, my kids and my work. Yet, it happened. A year later we were married. We started talking about doing medical missionary work in Africa since we were both Paramedics. I really felt a pull to serve God overseas using the talent I thought he had given me. I prayed more and believed more in God. I still didn't understand my prophetic gift, but knew it was from Him. I had begun filling out paperwork for the medical missionary trip. We had discussed the injections required, and the appointments were set to get everything rolling.

Just when I thought I was finally getting ahold of life, I got sick. I was newly married, mom of four, working two full time jobs, and every day it seemed like I was barely able to make it through the day. I began having terrible, debilitating headaches, but those were just the beginning. I was working as a paramedic on the ambulance as well as in the hospital emergency room. One day, while working a motor vehicle accident, I fell for no reason. I did not trip. It was as if my legs simply buckled underneath me and for about thirty seconds, I laid there on the ground in front of my colleagues and patient unable to move. As the days and weeks went on, I began having excruciating pain throughout my entire body. All of my joints, muscles, and bones hurt. I lost muscle control and strength. I was unable to sleep because the pain was so intense that lying down in my bed even hurt. I had such terrible fatigue it felt like I was trudging through mud wearing cast iron boots. Every day was a struggle. At my worst point I could not even raise my hands to wash my own hair. I saw many doctors and underwent more blood tests and imaging than I thought were possible. For months the best physicians I knew could not pinpoint why I was having so many problems. My inflammatory levels were through the roof. My liver functions were so out of whack they thought I had cancer. When all the test came in, they gave me a grim diagnosis and told me I would be dead before my thirty eighth birthday. At that moment the deepest depression set in. The friend that had invited me to church told me that she had a terrible dream about me. In the dream I was lying on the ground in a fetal position and there were many demons beating, hitting, and kicking me. Just as I would try to get up, they would increase the onslaught until I was just a crying heap on the floor. She was hesitant to tell me because she was unsure what all I really believed. I did not know what to think. I wasn't actively serving the Lord. At that time, I was attending church but had not fully committed my life to Christ. I believed he was my Lord and Savior, but I did not have a personal relationship with Him. I did not even pray and had no idea what the gifts of the spirit were. I was not even a lukewarm Christian. In all honesty, I was just going to church on Sunday to run from my checkered past.

My mother, on the other hand, was on fire for Jesus and had stepped into a whole new level of faith. I told her about the dream my friend had, and she didn't even bat an eye. She took me to see a man who was anointed in healing. Just before he prayed for me, this man, I had never met before, told me something with such power, authority and love. I stood there shocked and completely open to whatever he was going to pray because of this statement. He said, "Girl, God's gonna heal you. Not because of your faith because quite frankly, you have none, but because of your mother's. She has enough for both of you." He was absolutely right. From the moment he prayed for me, my spiritual life turned around. I experience the glory of God flowing over and through my body. I had never encountered God this way before. The immense warmth that overtook me was nearly indiscernible. I had never heard of being slain in the Spirit before, but God knocked me right off my high horse and into an old wooden church pew in the hallway of the sanctuary. Literally I felt God strike me in the top of my head so hard I was thrown back into the pew and knocked the pew up against the wall with a loud thud. Tears immediately began flowing down my cheeks. I looked up at this man of God and, full on snot crying, asked him why he had hit me. With love and understanding, and a bit of a chuckle, he told me he never touched me. I quickly looked over to my mother who was crying just as hard as I and asked her if he was telling the truth. She and many others confirmed this man was praying with his hand hovering about six inches from the top of my head when I had fallen. It was like God had hit my reset button.

When the shock wore off, I realized I had no pain. For this first time in three years, I could move my body without thinking I was going to die. I attended my first full gospel church service after I gained my composure enough to walk into the sanctuary. I heard about God the Father, Jesus, and the Holy Spirit like I had never heard of them before. I recommitted my life to Jesus that day. I repented for everything I had done. Not out of shame, but out of utter love and respect for my God.

I was excited to tell others about what had happened, and how God had healed me. My old friends were not so receptive though. I got laughed at many times for telling my testimony. Even though my doctors were confused when a week later I went in for my routine blood work and they could find literally nothing wrong with me, they still did not believe my healing was from God.

As the months progressed, I began to doubt it too. My unbelief caused pain to rise back up, but the doctors could still find nothing wrong. Yet, I was more inclined to believe them than the miracle I had witnessed with my own being.

Mark 16:17-18 (NKJV)

[17] And these signs will follow those who believe: In My name they will cast out demons; they will speak with new tongues; [18] they will take up serpents; and if they drink

anything deadly, it will by no means hurt them; they will lay hands on the sick, and they will recover."

One Day

I would love to say, that I moved on from there with greater faith and on fire for Jesus. I would love to say all that, but I can't, because it wouldn't be the truth. Life got twisted for me again when we had so many deaths in the family in a short amount of time.

John and I had been married now for two years. A solid year of that I had spent facing my own death. I really thought I knew my husband. We had so many intimate conversations. I never knew his full story. We had been so wrapped up in saving my own life and planning contingency plans for if we were unable to. I never realized I only thought I knew who he really was. He and I were both Paramedics, we were once partners on the ambulance. His father was a Paramedic, x-ray tech, respiratory tech, and dispatcher. He had trained me on the ambulance for critical care transports, and we worked together at the hospital. I was either in the Emergency Room or lab, and he was working x-ray. His mother a first-grade teacher. He had a brother who was retired from the military who was married, and they had a beautiful baby girl. I believed he was a medic. One of the best in the state. He still has calls that he handled so well that they now use to train the up and comers. It was true. He was all of that. However, there was more.

I walked into our home one day after my shift working in lab and John was sitting at our dining room table. He had no emotion on his face, just solace. He pushed the chair out across the table from where he was sitting with his long legs and motioned for me to sit. "Have a seat, we need to talk" he said. As I sat down looking into his piercing blue eyes, I could tell he was upset. The conversation that followed changed the course of our lives forever.

Leaning over on the table with his hands clasped tightly together, my husband of two years began telling me who he really was. "Grand mom died today." His words were flat and even. I told him I was so very sorry and started to get up and go hug him, and he just shook his head no at me. I had never seen him so intense.

Grand mom was John's dad's mother. She had fallen earlier that year and broken her hip. She was well on in age and had been a tough woman from all the stories I had heard. She was rough to some but was always wonderful to me. She had even hugged me the first time we met. I did not know her very well, but she was always kind to me. I assumed John was so upset that he had lost his grandmother, but there was so much more.

So, I sat back in my chair, and waited for the rest. He said, "you don't understand. Yes, it's sad she died, but I don't know how else to tell you the rest of this."

Okay, now I was worried. Thoughts were racing through my head. What could possibly be worse than a family member dying? How is there a worse? Our kids are fine, you're fine, I am fine. What is going on? Just as the panic reached my face he began. Head down, not looking straight at me anymore. He looked scared. Whatever he had to tell me was so hard for him to say. Panic left me, and all I could feel was deep compassion for the man I loved who was frightened to tell me something that was worse than a death.

"I am not who you think I am," he told me. "I am not just a paramedic, and I need you to really hear me out. Okay?"

Shock had set in at this point. I shook my head silently yes, and he continued.

"We are going to have to go Grand mom's funeral, and there are going to be a lot of other family there. People you have not met yet. Don't worry, they are harmless."

My head was spinning. What do you mean they are harmless? Like, why would I ever have doubted that? Internal freak out moment in 3….2….

"There's more." He continued. "My family has some land in this town we are going to for the funeral. While we are there, I want to go look at it. It's a ranch and it hasn't been lived on in quite some time. I haven't been there for about fifteen years. I really feel like, well, like we need to move there so we can take care of the ranch. It's what I was meant to do. I just know it. It may be a lot, but we can do this. I need to do this. What do you think?"

I was still in shock and thanking God my husband wasn't some government spy or something. It took me a few seconds to respond. I told him I had some questions and he replied okay with a shaky voice. I asked where in the world was this place, how big was it, and do you really feel like this is where you are supposed to be.

Almost timidly, he said "Well, it's in west Texas, it's about twenty-one sections and yes, I know that is what God wants me to do."

At least this place was still in my home state I thought. Let's see, twenty-one sections. I haven't heard of a section; surly he means acres. I told him about how I liked it was in west Texas and how much I had loved that area from when I went to college in Alpine. I proceeded to tell him that twenty-one acres would be no big deal. How we could do that. I had grown up on ten acres in northern central Texas. It would be just a bit bigger. We would have no problem with managing that. We could even put some cattle out there if he wanted. I was nervously going on and on when I saw him start laughing. Was he joking around? I know as medics we sometimes have a morbid sense of humor, but was he making all this up to make the blow of Grand mom dying easier for me. What is going on?

Laughing he said "No you, you don't understand. This is not twenty-one acres, honey. It's twenty-one sections. It's different. There are six hundred and forty acres to a section. It is one square mile per sections. The ranch is twenty-one square miles." Then still laughing he shook his head and murmured something about north Texas ranchers on acres of land and how I had no clue. Then he looked up at me, again with a fearful face and asked, "What do you think?".

I was in shock and my mind started reeling again. I was trying to comprehend a new language, a new way of seeing things. I couldn't imagine how big that was. I had no way to compare it to anything I knew before. He was passionate about it. What else could I have even possibly said other than let's do it? So, I looked him straight in the eye and said, "It sounds like a headache, a big headache, but if you feel like this is what you are supposed to do, then we will do it. You are my husband John; I go where you go. I do what you do."

He started to get up and walk around the table to me. He looked happier than I had seen him in a long time. Then he stopped. Halfway to me he said, "There's more."

I had it up to my eyeballs with that phrase. I was so overwhelmed with all this and what exactly this meant for our family. We were about to uproot the kids, move them across the state to a smaller west Texas town, and work on a ranch, and try to find a job as paramedics in a town that only had volunteer service. What on earth could he mean by more?

"There is more than one ranch," he said. "There's three, total, and we need to take care of all three."

I thought I was going to pass out. Who was this person? This paramedic from a family of paramedics. He was now a rancher, from a ranching family. Ranches, like three large areas of land to care for. Dear Lord. How are we going to do this? If this is what God wants him to do, then who am I to stand in the way of God.

I think I was silent for a few minutes trying to process everything. When the heavy silence was broken, all I could ask was; "Is there more?"

He answered. "No, not for now there is not more."

Questioning him one last time I asked; "John, why didn't you tell me about all of this before? Why did you wait? If this is what God wants you to do, and you feel that this strong, then why?"

With a love in his face I had never seen from him before he said simply; "I had to make sure you weren't with me because the ranches. I had to make sure you loved me for me and not for what I have."

I thought to myself, this man is insane. How could I not love him? We fought for my life together. I thought we had no secrets. He knew things about me that no one else would ever know. We didn't have anything but our love many times. I worked three different jobs, he worked two just to pay the bills and feed the kids. I loved him through all of that. Why would it make a difference if he had some land?

We shared a long embracing hug. One that said everything words cannot. Then, looking up into his eyes, I told him; "It's gonna be one heck of an adventure." Having no idea, the absolute truth to those words at the time we continued to talk about how this was going to be a whole new way of life for us and the kids.

There was no way to know just what God had instore for us. The death of a family member took us in a completely different direction than we had planned; than I had planned. How could we know that John's grandmother passing away would be the beginning of a chain of heartbreak, loss, rebuilding and new life.

Proverbs 3:5-6 New Living Translation (NLT)

⁵ Trust in the Lord with all your heart;
   do not depend on your own understanding.
⁶ Seek his will in all you do,
   and he will show you which path to take.

Seven Months

For the next several months after the death of Grand mom, our family was in paperwork turmoil. Closing estates from other family members, signing oil and gas leases, and finding lost property was taking a toll on everyone. John and his brother and parents were busier than ever making a game plan to keep everything rolling. The dynamic had changed. The family matriarch had died without having everything in order. There was much to be done and little time to do it all. My father in law took the heaviest burden from everyone else. That was always his job. He took care of all of us.

I met my father in law about a year before I had even met my husband. I had no idea he was even related to John for a long time. He trained me on the critical care unit. The amount of knowledge that man had was unbelievable. He was an amazing teacher. Patient and understanding of a clueless rookie like myself; he never seemed to get frustrated at the hundreds of questions I would ask in a shift. He would just answer and explain it again when I didn't understand. Years later after John and I married he treated me like his own daughter. That was just his way. He treated my sister in law the same way. He said he always wanted to have daughters and was so excited to have two in his life. It made him happy. For my thirtieth birthday, he and my mother in law gave me a surprise party. John was working offshore as a paramedic on a drilling rig. I had thought that I was going to have a quiet evening with the kids after I got off my shift from the lab. When I got home there was a huge banner strung across the front porch announcing my thirty years, and a wonderful taco bar and decorations throughout the house. There are countless other times where he showed how much he cared. He always made sure everyone had everything they needed. He loved to love on his family.

Then one day, seven months after his mother died, he had a massive pulmonary embolism. He was gone. It seemed like time stopped. None of us were prepared. We were all in shock. The next few weeks went by as if they were in slow motion. Funeral arrangements were made, and then put into action. There were so many people who attended his funeral I had never met before. Some family. Most friends. All knew just how amazing of a man he was.

With my father in law gone, the strain of keeping the ranches, that had been in the family for over a hundred years, up and running, fell on my husband and his brother Jason. My mother in law, Kay, was in such a dark emotional place that she was not able to truly pick up the entirety of the reins. So, John and Jason split the responsibilities. John's job was the land and the livestock. Jason's was the oil and gas paperwork and negotiating new leases. Both also took care of Kay and helped her along the way. It was like new jobs were handed out almost instantly, and John and I moved across Texas to work on the ranch.

Before we had completely moved, we made a big family decision. We all sat down at Jason's house and incorporated the ranches under the guise of always being above board and doing business in a Godly manner. This was a resolute decision, spoken out by Kay, the new matriarch of the family. A deeply profound moment where God had led her through her grief to make a covenant with the Father. An unwavering statute that remains to this day.

We embarked into the unknown that day. As Jason battled oil and gas companies, John and I battled against livestock that had been left virtually unattended for nearly twenty years.

We built much of the exterior fence lines with rolls of bailing or tie wire, and a pair of plyers. The pens that would have been used to round up cows and goats for care and sale were seemingly gone. The bulls were so unruly and wild, that we found ourselves literally running for our lives away from them when trying to get them into a trailer for sale. These massive Charolais brahma cross bulls put us over the fence more times than I can even remember. It seemed like they were out to kill us, and had it not been for some miraculous events, they would have succeeded. In a short amount of time we were left with yet another death in the family.

Numbers 10:9 New Living Translation (NLT)

[9] *"When you arrive in your own land and go to war against your enemies who attack you, sound the alarm with the trumpets. Then the Lord your God will remember you and rescue you from your enemies.*

Two Years

Jason was strong and a fighter. He was one of the youngest green berets in military history. He always said he was a born soldier. Although he had been out of the army for a while before I met him, he always carried that intensity. Every negotiation he entered was like a new battle ground. He had a cogency plan for scenarios I would have never even dreamt were possible. He was also fun and caring. Many times, when John was working offshore, Jason would come by the house to check on the kids and I. The only agenda was to make sure his brother's wife and children didn't need anything. Often, he would bring candy or gifts for the kids and would sit and visit for a few minutes before heading home. Jason loved his wife and daughter fiercely. He would move the moon if they asked him to, just to see them smile. Everything he worked on was done one hundred percent. There was no half doing anything. It was all or nothing and done correctly every time. Jason held himself to a higher standard. Things were either done right or not at all.

It didn't take long until the mounting stress and problems from a life lived post war would claim its victim. Just over two years, from the death of my father in law, John's brother Jason died from an internal hemorrhage. We were all left once again, in utter and complete shock. Jason was only thirty-one years old. His young wife, and five-year-old daughter, were suddenly alone.

John and I were left to carry the burden that neither Kay or Jason's wife were in a position to carry along with us. Before his death, Jason had completed much of the oil and gas paperwork. Thankfully all his efforts, and my father in law before him, had made it where John and I neither had to work another outside job. We could focus on the land and livestock. As well as focus on Kay, and making sure we didn't lose her as well.

The resolve and strength of my mother in law, paired with the love and undeniable commitment to the Lord carried the rest of the broken remnants of our family.

Three deaths. A different life. In a whole new place. In less than three years.

Isaiah 40:29 New Living Translation (NLT)

[29] *He gives power to the weak*
and strength to the powerless.

Chapter Two: Fighting for Freedom

Romans 8:1-4 (NKJV)

8 There is therefore now no condemnation to those who are in Christ Jesus, who do not walk according to the flesh, but according to the Spirit. ² For the law of the Spirit of life in Christ Jesus has made me free from the law of sin and death. ³ For what the law could not do in that it was weak through the flesh, God did by sending His own Son in the likeness of sinful flesh, on account of sin: He condemned sin in the flesh, ⁴ that the righteous requirement of the law might be fulfilled in us who do not walk according to the flesh but according to the Spirit.

John and I were fighting not only for our physical lives, but for our spiritual and emotional ones as well. We had been through so much over the last three years. Exhausted with grief, but unable to slow down for even a moment to process the previous events, we pushed through. There always seemed to be something new to fight around every corner. My first face to face experiences with demonic entities were almost too much to bear.

The spiritual warfare started just after the death of my father in law, when John and I moved to the ranch. We had started attending a local church regularly. I was still battling myself to believe the full and complete healing God had given me in the years prior to our move. I would have increased pain, depression and anxiety. I also started having vivid dreams and visions. God was slowly growing my prophetic gift. He showed me many visions and gave me numerous words of knowledge of things that have come to pass within the last ten years. It seemed though something else was attempting to crack into my head and show me terrible visons.

Nightmares became almost a nightly experience. I suffered from night terrors so horrible that I would not sleep many hours unless it was during the day. It didn't take long before I wasn't the only one effected by these bad dreams. First it was John. Then the kids started having them too. John would dream of gory and gruesome fights. Things not even found in horror movies. These were more than your normal nightmare type of dream. They pushed constant thoughts of anger and violence in haunting images that remained long after waking. When it began, we believed it was due to all the stress we had been under. The more we tried to ignore them the worse they seemed to get. Bloodier, angrier and more terrifying. Until demonic entities began manifesting in our dreams. Horrible disfigured beings lurked and would attack us during our sleep. The most terrible ones would occur when they would try to catch us off guard. One such dream haunted me for years, and has become a reoccurring nightmare.

It always starts out the same. Just as I am starting to fall asleep, I feel who I think is my husband cuddle up next to me at my back. He wraps his arms around me for an embrace but his arms become heavy. Just as I tell him goodnight, he replies with a voice that starts out sounding like John, but the tone is off. He says, "Oh, it's going to be a good night, but you are not going to sleep." I start to struggle to break free, but his arms around me are heavy and strong. Just as I start to try and punch and kick my way out, he flips me over onto my back and holds me down. I can't move. I can't wake up. I can't scream. Suddenly other beings, appearing more mangled humans start to surround me. With heinous laughter and hissing they start beating me as I lay there frozen except for my thoughts. I finally break free and sit straight up in bed, fully awake, shaking and covered in cold sweat. Just as I begin to fall back asleep the entire cycle begins again. Usually they are all just there waiting to pounce on me and hold me down where I cannot fight back. By the fifth or sixth time of the cycle, I am finally able to speak. I scream for them to leave in the name of Jesus. They finally do leave and I will be able to sleep sound.

I would say this would be a night terror attack except sometimes it starts after I have fallen asleep. I am in another dream and they show up and attack. The main difference between when this was happening in the past and when they try now is, I know before hand when this attack is coming. I am prepared and ready to fight in the name of Jesus before they ever incapacitate me. Back then, however, I didn't know how to fight them. I would tell myself that this was just all in my head. Nightmares can't hurt you, right?

Soon enough I found they could. I would wake in the morning with large unexplained bruises and scratches. These marks would appear in places that were difficult for me to reach like the middle of my back. When you are going through those type of things you try to find a way to rationalize the experience. I would tell myself, it's just a bad dream, or I must have hit something the day before and not realized it. My mind wanted to deny what I was feeling in my spirit. I couldn't or didn't want to think that a physical attack could come from a dream. For a few weeks, things were quiet. No bad dreams and no marks were had. That was just the calm before the storm.

Ephesians 6:12 (NKJV)

¹² For we do not wrestle against flesh and blood, but against principalities, against powers, against the rulers of the darkness of this age, against spiritual hosts of wickedness in the heavenly places.

Miserable to Miraculous

Coming to a new town was difficult. We had gone from living in a small central Texas city, to the middle of the ranch. Our closest neighbor is over seven miles away through pasture land. I was in shell shock. I had no idea how to be a ranching wife. I would help out as much as I could, but all I knew how to do was be a paramedic or work in a store front. I cried every night for six months. No one in town would talk to me because I was an outsider. I had no friends, no one at church really even spoke to me. Aside of the friends John had from high school and their spouses, I didn't know anyone. I prayed and begged God to take us away from this place, from the stress of the ranch and unruly livestock, and from people who obviously wanted nothing to do with me.

I had gone from working three full time jobs to being at home all day. There was not much for me to do on the ranch because it was far too dangerous. You can only clean house so much before it is done. I was lonely and going a little stir crazy being cooped up all the time. Until one day I decided on a whim to open a business. I was making all-natural soaps and lotions from the house. The business grew and eventually I rented commercial space in town to open a storefront. Determined to work hard, and meet more people who would hopefully accept me for me. I did it. I started to get to know people from town and make some new friends. God slowly started working on my attitude towards our entire situation. Things were getting crazier and crazier at the ranch, but in my shop, there was peace. I didn't tell anyone what was going on. I had barely gotten these people to start talking to me. I was afraid that if I told them they would think I was super crazy. So, I would push it aside while working, and just focus on people. I struggled for a while, but as the days turned into months, I found more peace with living in such a secluded area. I had stopped crying about being here. Then one day, out of the blue I met an angel.

My storefront was in an old building with large glass front that overlooked the town square. Decorated with shelving made from repurposed wood and wire from the ranch, and a large stage with an old cast iron claw foot bathtub in front of the large windows, showed a country chic boutique. It was a perfect place to attract many people who were passing through our small town via the interstate. I had more customers from other places than from the locals. Especially during the summer, when west Texas is blazing three digits hot; many travelers would stop to walk around the town square park and wander into my business to cool off. I kept a refrigerator with bottled water stocked for that particular reason. When a new face walked in my door, I was excited to meet people from all over the world. It was not odd to have men and women alike just stopping by because they had seen the bathtub in the window. So, when a man I had never met before walked in, on a day when I had not had many customers, I assumed he was one of those new faces. But he was different.

The temperature that day was well into the nineties. I was looking out the windows from across the room, but never noticed him walking up to the door; until it opened. He was average height and build. He was wearing a long sleeve black button up shirt with the sleeves rolled up to the elbow, tucked into black jeans, with a black belt and silver buckle. Around his neck was a leather cord with a worn wooden thick cross. I welcomed him as I did all my customers, with a warm hello, my name and let me know if you need help finding anything. He replied with a complementary warm hello, and asked how I was doing. After our exchange of pleasantries, I realized he must be hot wearing all black on such a sweltering day. Walking over to the mini refrigerator I asked if he would like a bottle of water. He politely said "yes please, and a conversation. If you don't mind?" I responded with an of course, and pointed to the small table with two chairs sitting beside the wall. As we sat down, I noticed his beautiful olive skin tone and thick black hair that framed his fierce blue eyes. He had a kind smile and a demeanor that was comfortable to be around. After taking a long drink of water, he thanked me for offering him, and told me he had been on quite the journey. Before I could ask where he was coming from or headed to, he asked me a question.

"Are you happy here?" he asked.

"Sure" I replied.

With a questioning look to his face, he began asking questions about our small town. He asked me what the people here were like, and if I thought this was a good place to live. I told him "the people here are great. They are west Texas tough, and weren't all so easy to get to know at first, but given some time, they really are some of the best people I had ever met."

"Really? Well, do you like this town in general?" he inquired.

I couldn't help but be completely honest with this guy. It was as if I was unable to sugar coat anything. I had to give him a straight forward answer. I unapologetically began telling him everything I like about our town and more. "I didn't like it at first here. It was hard for me being so secluded and no one would even talk to me. But now, I have gotten know more people and they are really great. Once you get passed the tough façade, the people here are good hearted. They love their families like crazy, and if you are good to them, they are good right back. They treat you as family once they know you. It's a great place to raise a family." Realizing I had been rambling I stopped to take a drink of my water and try and collect my thoughts.

He questioned me again saying, "are you happy here, what else is interesting about this town?"

Answering again without a filter, I said "I am happy here. There are some funny quirks here, like most towns, but truly it's a beautiful place to be."

After him asking for an example, I walked over to the window, motioning for him to follow as I pointed to the far side of the park, and said "even the statue over there has an interesting story, like most of the people here."

He shook his head in agreement and said "let's go look at it."

"Sure, let's go. You up for a walk? I could use one." I rambled on again.

Then I walked out of my shop, leaving the door wide open, with no one else there, with a perfect stranger. Chatting the whole way, I told him how our town had received the statue by mistake, but because it would have been too expensive to ship to its rightful place, the other city had allowed us to keep it here. I went on to tell him how travelers from all over come to take a picture with a piece of town history. When we reached the statue, he read the plaque, chuckled, and we began our walk back. He told me how interesting he saw of the dynamics of our little unincorporated town is. As we walked back into the store, I offered him another bottle of water for the road. He gladly accepted the water, and then asked me a third time, "are you happy here?" I answered him with an enthusiastic "Yes" Then he told me that he had better be going because he still had a long journey ahead and that he was really glad that I was enjoying this place so much.

Just before he walked out the door, I came to the realization I had never gotten his name, so I asked. He said, "my name is Michael." Then he turned and walked out the door, and straight down across the park we had just came from. I watched as he walked halfway back to the statue we had just visited, and then in an instant, he was gone. Vanished into thin air.

In that instant, I knew I had just met an angel. God spoke straight to my heart and I dropped to my knees and cried like a baby; completely overwhelmed with emotion and knowing that if I had answered his question differently, he would have moved me to somewhere else.

To this day I am humbled and thank my Lord, that He would think enough of the wailings from before to send an angel, to move me if I was not able to be happy. That God could love me, even though I wasn't serving him and was in no way worthy. I learned the truth of His grace that day. When I feel like God is not hearing my prayers, I remember that day and the utter proof He gave me of His love, grace and patience.

Hebrews 13:2 (KJV)

2 Be not forgetful to entertain strangers: for thereby some have entertained angels unawares.

Strange Activity

I honestly believed things were looking better. After meeting Michael, I had a renewed hope. My faith was elevated through the experience, but it didn't take long for that to change. My mother in law invited me to go with her to a church conference out of state and I thought this would be a good way to learn more about my Heavenly Father. It was a prophetic conference, and I had been having some amazing prophetic dreams and visions. I believed that I would gain insight about my gifting. As it turned out, I wasn't there to receive training on my gift. What I did learn was more about my savior, the bible and the Word of God. I listened to some of the greatest preachers and teachers of our time talking about God, Jesus, and the Holy Spirit like I had never heard before. Wisdom flowed straight out of these men and women and I was like a sponge trying to soak up every word. I was seeing things in such a different perspective that I did not even know was possible. It seemed as much as I started to study and learn more of God's Word, the more intense things were happening at home.

It started small at first. There were strange things happening that we couldn't explain but we were so busy with cleaning up the livestock and the old barns that we didn't pay attention. I would come in the house and put my keys on the kitchen bar and the next day they would be gone. I would spend a bunch of time looking for them knowing I had set them in the same spot I always had only to find the keys on a shelf in the closet. I would think that I must have been too tired and set them in there for some reason. Seemed legitimate, except it kept happening day after day. John would laugh and say to the kids something like let's find mom's keys again guys. They would end up in the strangest of places such as on top of the refrigerator, outside in the yard, in the washing machine, under the couch and even in the pantry. For a while I assumed that my kids were hiding them from me just to play a joke. They assured me that was not the case, although they wished they would have thought to do it because it would have been funny.

After the keys stopped going missing, weird noises began. We had remodeled the old ranch house, so I thought the noises were just from the house settling. They got louder and less random. Every night at eleven o'clock on the dot, there would be a loud crack sound in the front hallway, followed by a thud sound in the main living room. This went on for months. You could set a watch by its timing. When the crack and thud first started, I tried to rationalize that the sounds were coming from the metal roof flexing from the hot temperatures of day to the cooler night. That is, until I realized they were so perfectly timed.

Next, it was loud knocking sounds all around the main living room. Two or three knocks on each wall in the same order every night after the crack and thud. It never failed, after the knocks going from east, west, south, and then north, it sounded as if something had fallen in the kitchen and broken. Like the sound of broken glass. I would go and turn on the lights and search, but never found anything broken. Several weeks went by and the sound of breaking glass changed to loud clamoring as if someone had dropped all the pots and pans onto the floor. Again, after checking, nothing was out of place.

After this there was a beeping sound. It was a high pitched, ding-dong pattern that was added to the nightly events. After a couple of days of waiting and searching for the sound I found it. In our back hallway we have a full-size refrigerator that stays stocked with bottled water, Gatorade. and sodas we call it our drink fridge. It has one of those ice and water dispensers in the door of the freezer which hold all manner of pop cycles and ice cream treats. The water and ice maker is not hooked up to a water source, so we just leave the button set to off. This button, however, was the source of the beeping sound. I walked to the back hall during one of the more dramatic, almost frantic, fast paced beeping to see the indicator for the ice changing from off, to cubed ice then to crushed ice and back to off. I pressed the button and the refrigerator sounded the same sound I had been hearing, and I continued until I had cycled it back to the off position. Once I put my hand back down to my side it would start again. Then, every time I would reach to touch the button again it would stop, but when I would put my hand back down, it would start up again.

The sound grated on my nerves and made me anxious and honestly freaked out. The hair on my arms would stand on edge and my head would ache as if it was being squeezed in a vice. Out of aggravation I would yell at the refrigerator to stop. I told John that I thought it was having electrical problems, but the only electrical thing that was going crazy was the ice button. It was not stuck, and after about thirty minutes every night after the crack, thud, breaking sounds, it would beep. Then it was quiet. All of this had become some common place that we started ignoring it. It was just part of our normal life.

After many months, things got more and more intense. The front and back door, despite being locked, would open and close with a loud slam. John would jump up and go check to make sure we did not have some uninvited guest showing up, or that the large dogs we had didn't knock open the door trying to get in. He began checking, and rechecking to make sure everything was locked up before we went to bed. By this time our nerves were seriously on edge.

Many nights, we would lay down and be just about asleep before the doors would do their thing. Right after John would rush to check and see everything was still locked up tight, he would lay back down, and the next spine-chilling noise would happen. It sounded as if a large dog was walking down the front hallway. We would hear the clip of nails on the hardwood floor. Tapping from the front door, down the hallway, across the main living room, and stopping at the door to our bedroom. We had two German Shepherd dogs at the time, and this sounded much heavier than them.

Sleeping was difficult to say the least. It only seemed to happen out of sheer exhaustion. I would get so tired that I would sleep during the day while the kids were at school. When I would try to sleep at night the night terrors and nightmares would plague me. They became worse and more violent and even perverse. It was like being tortured every night. We were getting weary and worn down from the constant mental abuse these sounds and nightmares caused. It started affecting our daughter, Dacie. She would have scary, bad dreams as well. I thought it couldn't get any worse, but I could never have been so wrong. It got worse, much worse.

Activity outside the house began to spin up as well. Living in such an isolated area you get used to the nature noises around you pretty quick. These were far from natural occurrences. Many times, I would hear a child screaming and would even hear this same childlike voice shouting my name. I would run to check on the kids, but it was not them. The scream would run chills up and down my spine. Although I could never find the source of the blood curdling shout of an unknown child, I felt it best to stop searching. Standing in the cattle pens we began hearing people talking and yelling. This escalated into hearing the gates open and close and the sounds of cattle and horses got so loud you would think there was a group of five to six men working a load of cows via horseback. As impressive as this was, it wasn't scary.

1 Peter 5:8 (NLT)

[8] Stay alert! Watch out for your great enemy, the devil. He prowls around like a roaring lion, looking for someone to devour.

Chapter Three: Full Attack

John 16:33 (NKJV)

³³ These things I have spoken to you, that in Me you may have peace. In the world you will have tribulation; but be of good cheer, I have overcome the world."

Broken down from the daily mental assault, I tricked myself into thinking that what we were experiencing was the worst of it. Our emotional strain worsened when John's brother Jason died after almost a year of the constant nightly rounds of the unexplained sounds. That's when all hell truly broke loose inside and outside our home.

The first night the activity picked up, I was standing in my bedroom looking out the large double window that overlooks our driveway into the main working pens about one hundred yards away. I kept hearing muffled sounds of men yelling and I was looking to see who could be out so late. Living in a remote area in south west Texas, it was not uncommon for us to have illegal immigrants frequently crossing our land. Because the house had been vacant for so long, it had been used by these people as a stopping point for many years. Most of the time they wouldn't come directly to the house once they noticed someone was living here. It had happened on occasion, but they were never loud. They did not want to be noticed, so they would rarely ever speak and if they did it was barely louder than a whisper. So muffled yelling was out of the ordinary. I kept thinking someone must have been hurt and they were trying to get our attention regardless of what it would have meant. I saw no one. John walked all around the barns and pens looking but couldn't find anyone. More than that, he couldn't hear any of the yelling that was so audible from inside our bedroom. It didn't make sense how it sounded like it was coming from outside, but out of the house was completely quiet.

Suddenly, the shouting got much louder and distinguishable. We could hear someone yelling instructions to other men as if they were loading a herd of cattle into the pens. The half English half Spanish words were clear and distinct. John and I quickly went outside and by the time we got to the driveway we could hear many different voices. They were saying things like move them here, now hurry and shut the gate, or go grab that calf and get it in the squeeze chute. It was like hearing an old wild west round up movie with no picture. Especially when we could hear the gates moving, slamming shut, and the distinct sound of the squeeze chute operating open and closed. Just when we began walking slowly to the pens, in utter shock, we heard the cattle and horses.

Living on a cattle ranch you learn fairly quickly that cattle make many different types of noises. When they are content, they lo, or make a soft mooing sound. When a calf is separated from its mother it moos with a crying desperation sound and when a calf is taken away from its mother the cow will stay for about three days making saddened low tone mooing sounds like weeping. Cattle make a completely different sound when being worked through the pens. Shorter mooing and almost huffing noises resonate along with the thundering sound of many heavy hooves against the ground.

The latter was what we were hearing. By the time we walked into the pens we began seeing them. John turned on the bright pen lights and you could see an entire herd of spectral cattle moving through the staging pens. Dust started flying up from the ground as the cows hurried from pen to pen. I stood frozen watching as a man riding a horse yelling and swinging a tie rope came running towards me at full steam. I didn't know what to expect. It was like watching a transparent image completely effect the area around it. They ran through trees, not around them. So, I stood there as this horseback ghost ran toward me. I assumed they would go around or just pass by me and I would not feel a thing. By the time it reached me I could smell the livestock and all the hair on my arms stood on end. Then it struck. I was pushed backwards hard enough that I fell straight onto my back with a loud thud. I felt like I had just been run over by a horse. Not some floating ghost, but an actual live massive horse.

John ran over to where I was now laying on the loosened dirt. He helped me to my feet and we just stared at each other for a moment trying to grasp what had happened. Just then, the overhead light went out with a flicker. We were standing in the dark before we realized it was completely quiet. No sounds, no sights, no dust flying up, and no smell. A strong wind picked up and started moving an open gate enough to make a tapping sound from the swinging lock chain bumping the fence beside it.

We joked with each other saying that it was too bad those ghost cowboys were not able to work our live cows for us. At least those crazy cows and bull wouldn't be able to kill those guys. The humor broke the tension long enough for us to get back inside to try and sleep. Little did we know what was to come.

1 Corinthians 15:58 (NLT)

[58] So, my dear brothers and sisters, be strong and immovable. Always work enthusiastically for the Lord, for you know that nothing you do for the Lord is ever useless.

Markings and Mysterious Sickness

The ghost cowboys went on nightly for about two weeks and then started occurring only once or twice a week. Always after eleven o'clock in the evening. We tried to tell some of our friends what was happening, but they didn't believe us. We were told we were simply over exaggerating and that we must have not been used to the hard winds that could swirl up that made all kinds of howling sounds and move gates. Not a single person we told took us seriously. After a month of trying to get someone to listen we just stopped saying anything. John and I decided that maybe those people were right, and we were just too exhausted to think about it rationally. What were we going to do about all of that anyway? It stopped completely in about two months, so we put it out of our heads and focused on completing the remodeling of the pens and barns.

For a while we had a reprieve from all the weird noises and working men. About two weeks after the last roundup we thought we had put all that craziness behind us. Suddenly, without notice, it happened. John was coming out of the master bathroom after a shower and started complaining about how his back felt like it was on fire. I raised his shirt and there were large, deep, bleeding scratches running from his left shoulder across his back to his right hip. Three in all, in a continuous line that he could in no way have made himself. Trying again to make sense of it, I asked if he had brushed up against a mesquite tree with those long thorns while he was outside working. John reassured me that he didn't remember being scratched by anything. Besides, if he had they wouldn't be so bloody after his shower. His work shirt had no rips, tears or blood on or in it. We just tried to let it go. That night was full of the horrendous nightmares again. This time however, an entity spoke directly to me.

It was tall and dark with a long thick black hooded robe that met the floor. Long bell sleeves covered thin boney arms and half of its skeleton like hands. The hood covered most of its face, but I could still see the hollow solid black eyes staring back at me. It was expressionless except for the slight smirk after it spoke. Pointing at me with a crooked boney finger it said, "I was sent here to kill you.

I had heard this phrase said directly to me from a patient I once had when working the ambulance. This person, however, grabbed me by my throat and had slammed me up against the wall of the ambulance as he screamed it into my face. Had an officer not showed up on the scene I believed this person would have succeeded their mission. Although that had been several years earlier, I felt the similarity in my gut. The eyes were the same. Hollow, black and soulless.

I awoke in a cold sweat and gasping for air. Immediately my entire body was in immense pain. I had a hard time moving as every joint felt like it was grating hard against itself. Laying back down on my soft bed was even painful. My skin felt as if I had been severely sunburned and as if I was covered in mosquito bites on top of it. I took a couple of deep breaths and closed my eyes but couldn't fall back asleep. My heart was racing. I was just too worked up. So, I got out of bed and went into the living room where I finally fell asleep as the sun was just coming up.

The next few nights were plagued with nightmares of physically fighting off demons. I would wake in the morning to find bruises on my body and scratch marks I couldn't account for. One night in particular I dreamt something had ahold of my arm. I was being dragged out of bed by the upper part of my left arm. There was something I could not totally see with a large scaly hand wrapped completely around my bicep, trying to drag me out of bed. When I awoke the next morning, I had bruises that would have matched where it had grabbed me. Not only that, I was half off the bed on my upper body left side. I was sore and exhausted.

Maybe it was all the battles in my dreams, or maybe it was because I was so mentally tired, but I started getting sick again. It was like before. Everything started to hurt. As badly as I was starting to feel, the attacks on my husband increased. He started getting run down too and was marked with scratches on almost a daily basis. His body hurt too, but he couldn't stop working. He was fighting to keep the ranch going. There was no choice.

This went off and on for months. There were brief periods when we would have nothing happening, followed by an onslaught of what we thought at the time was the worst things to go through. We had no idea then how bad things really could be.

John started having a lot of pain in his abdomen. After a visit to our local doctor we found he had a hernia that needed to be repaired. In a short couple of weeks, he had surgery on an umbilical hernia. It was a day surgery, so we were able to come home for his recovery as long has he made his appointments with the doctor an hour away. We were walking out the back door to the car for his first follow up appointment when near disaster struck. John was about to step outside of the house when I stopped at the drink fridge to grab us a couple of drinks for the drive. Just as I opened the door to the refrigerator, I saw my husband falling forward. His hands that were holding a pillow to his stomach were flailed behind him. His back was arched forward and both legs were off the ground headed straight back behind him. One of our German Shepherd dogs apparently saw him and instinctively ran underneath him to brace his fall. I rushed over to help him to his feet still trying to figure out what I had just witnessed.

It didn't look like he had tripped. He had been pushed. How was that even possible I kept asking myself. As soon as I reached him, he looked straight up at me with such sadness and asked me, "why did you push me?" I implored him that I had not touched him. I showed him where I was standing. The door to the refrigerator was still standing open. There was no way I could have been there and even remotely reached him by the door.

Throughout the entire one-hour drive to the doctor we talked about the incident. Trying to rationalize what had happened and how he could have been pushed so fiercely was a complete mystery. Upon seeing the doctor, we had told him that John had fallen, but did not hit the ground because of our dog. The doctor then informed us that had John actually landed on the concrete on his surgical site that things would have been extremely bad. He could have literally started bleeding internally and would not have had enough time to get to a doctor for the repair. He could have died.

At this point we realized how serious things were at the house. We had just thought it was us just being overly sensitive or stressed. We had thought that we were possibly just seeing or hearing things. We thought that all the nightmares were just our own subconscious living out scenarios due to high levels of stress and grief. That fall. That push was our wakeup call. We had to act. But how? No one knew about what was happening. We had tried to tell people before but were basically told we were making it all up. There was no reason to tell anyone about it; they wouldn't believe us anyway.

Things got quiet around the house then. John recovered and we started to find some normalcy to life. He worked outside on the ranch and I had my shop in town. All was good for about two months. Then, the unseen decided to show itself.

1 Corinthians 16:13 (NLT)

[13] *Be on guard. Stand firm in the faith. Be courageous. Be strong.*

Seeing is Believing

The eleven o'clock nightly sounds happened as usual except after the crashing of dishes there was someone standing in our kitchen. An old woman. She would stand there for a couple of seconds before walking into the dining room and then was gone. She was wearing a long white gown with short sleeves. She had no expression on her face, just a blank stare. That look was enough. Over time we would see her sitting on the end of the couch or walking through the dining room heading toward the back door. Her presence was very unsettling. Even past the initial startle factor of seeing a full-bodied ghost standing in the house; it was eerie. Like being punched in the gut.

After her was a man that started showing up. He never spoke or made an expression either. He wore blue jeans with a red t-shirt and a baseball cap. Sometimes he would be standing in the main living room. Others he would be walking around the outside of the house. There would always be that same ugly feeling in the pit of my stomach every time he was around.

The worst feeling came when I saw the little girl. She was wearing a long white dress or nightgown with ruffles at the ankles. She had long dark wavy hair. Her expression was different from the others. She would smile and giggle. Her smile was mischievous. It was more of a half smirk or fake smile. This little girl ghost would dance and twirl around in the dining room and then half run into the back hallway. As soon as she wasn't visible anymore the refrigerator would start beeping. On days I was inside the house by myself preparing supper for the family I would catch her out of the corner of my eye. Then the beeping would start. This was usually around four thirty in the afternoon. The beeping continued for the entire time I would be in the kitchen. It was that little girl that gave me the worst feeling of all. It just felt evil.

After her appearance it seemed like many other strange events started happening. More noises, more apparitions, more night terrors and nightmares and more scratches and bruises. I got pushed out of the shower, pushed backwards while standing in the kitchen trying to cook and glasses would fall out of the cabinet on top of me and break. I started hearing screams in a girl's voice that sounded like my daughter. I would rush to find Dacie fast asleep in bed. Sometimes, it would happen during the day and when Dacie was at school.

We tried to keep everything from the kids as much as possible. It was difficult for them with having nightmares too. More than that, it was hard for them seeing John and I so stressed. We would argue a lot, and often it seemed like we could not agree on anything. We had to stay focused on fighting the feelings and emotions of anger towards each other. The kids didn't deserve to see us like that. Our home had always been built on love and communication, even though disagreements. We tried to find ways to bring joy and laughter back into our home.

No one has ever claimed that our family has been normal. That's just not who we are. We don't fit into the socially accepted box of normality. So, the ways we found to bring that joy back were not normal either. Many times, during the hot Texas summer we would have water fights. Sometimes we would use water balloons or water guns, but there were a few occurrences of running through the house with a water hose spraying each other and the entire house. The little spray nozzle on the sink in the kitchen was also a well-used prank. The handle would get stuck just enough so when you turned on the faucet you would get a spray in the face. Pitchers of water were also formidable weapons when poured over the unexpecting recipient. During one of these water fights, our youngest son ran into the house with the sprinkler we were using to water the lawn, on full blast. We and the entire floor of the house were soaked. Instead of getting upset at the amount of cleanup we knew we were all in for, we would just laugh and then clean up the house. Although fairly unconventional methods of summer fun, our floors were usually very clean.

All of us worked hard on the ranch and played hard too. On weekends our two oldest sons would have friends out and we would barbeque and have a fire pit going. Many of those nights we would sit out and they would play guitars and sing for hours. The next morning all of us would be working in the pens catching goats and having our own goat roping contest. Oddly enough, our two youngest would rope the biggest goats and be holding on for dear life as John or I could make it over to get them undone. Once, Dacie roped two very large Spanish Boer Billy goats together in one loop. These types of goats have large horns almost thirty inches from head to tip and weigh over a hundred pounds. She was in middle school at the time and didn't weigh as much as one of those big Billie's herself. Dacie won that contest that day as she laughed running behind those two goats, trying to stay on her feet, as they struggled to get free.

Moments like those became essential for our emotional survival during the entire ordeal. It became essential for us to find joy in the small things too. Although the laughter seemed fleeting, it kept us from becoming so bogged down. It gave us hope that we could laugh through the pain and gave the kids a chance to just be kids. The attacks were still there, but the fun and laughter were like a soothing balm that brought some relief. We still had to find a way to truly handle our attacks.

Nehemiah 8:10 (AMPC)

[10] *Then [Ezra] told them, go your way, eat the fat, drink the sweet drink, and send portions to him for whom nothing is prepared; for this day is holy to our Lord. And be not grieved and depressed, for the joy of the Lord is your strength and stronghold.*

The Last Straw

After years of attacks we had become completely worn down. We became chronically sick with something. Sinus infections, migraine headaches, severe chest colds, and continuous bodily pain just to name a few. Then there were injuries from mysterious falls or complete loss of balance. We were ragged and tired all the time. John and I started arguing more and more. Emotionally torn, we began yelling instead of communicating with each other. It was like we felt completely unwanted in our own home. Unwanted by each other, the livestock, the house itself and our exile just made things worse. The last night that things got really bad still gives me chills.

John and I had been arguing all day. We went to bed especially exhausted even considering the last couple of years events. That night had taken an emotional toll on both of us. We said goodnight to each other and decided we would talk more about everything in the morning. The nightmares started immediately for me. It was the same being held down and beaten ferociously with no escape. Only this time I kept hearing screams that again sounded like my daughter. I was shaken awake by John grabbing me and yelling "no!" He had ahold of my shirt with one hand and was sitting straight up in bed. With his other hand, it looked as though he was holding or pushing something back away from us. When I finally could see in the swirling pitch black room, I realized there was something standing at Johns side of the bed reaching for him. It was huge, at least seven-foot-tall and a swirling mass of dark fluttering wings. The stench that filled the air I can only say smelled like rotten flesh and mildew at the same time. There was another loud shrill scream coming from this figure that made our blood run cold. I exclaimed "Oh my God! John what is going on?"

Suddenly, the swirling mass burst into hundreds of moths. They filled our entire bedroom, bathroom, main living room, kitchen and dining room. John jumped up out of bed and told me to check on the kids. I ran out of the room and across our house to the kid's bedrooms. They were all peacefully asleep. None of them even awoke when I opened their doors, walked in and placed my hands on them. I made my way back to the other side of the house where my husband was armed with the shop vac and a flashlight. He held the light on the end of the hose and as the moths were drawn to it, he vacuumed them up to their deaths. The foul smell started to fade, but the terror didn't. We filled and emptied the large shop vacuum four times that night.

As the sun started to come up, we were still cleaning the mess of dead moths from house. There were so many that had landed on the walls that we had to wash all of them and then later repaint what they had destroyed. Still shaking from what had happened John and I were trying to figure out what we were going to do. All of the past few years' events had culminated into a being trying to grab my husband out of bed. Enough was enough. This was obviously a full demonic attack, but who would believe us?

John called the pastor at the church we were attending at the time. I sat and listened as my husband explained everything that had happened. He told them about the noises, the apparitions and the moth man from the night before. John was calm and didn't show any heightened emotion when he was telling the preacher all the events. He was very matter of fact. Then I could hear the preacher say a few words I couldn't believe. He said, "well, I'll be praying for you, but I don't know what else to do." John looking defeated just said an okay and thank you as he hung up the phone.

We were plagued for the entire month with a moth infestation. As soon as the sun would go down, we turned off all lights in the house. John duct taped the flashlight to the vacuum hose aimed at one of the recessed can lights. As bad as these bugs were in the house, the attic was one hundred times worse. They would come into the house from those lights every night after dark. We called exterminators who told us there was nothing they could really do, and that we just had to wait it out. The entire east side of our house on the outside had turned from the yellow color it was to a black and brown stained mess. We had to sleep with the covers pulled completely over our heads and tucked in. If not, moths would fly into our faces continuously. For a month there was no reprieve.

What little sleep we did get was infested with continued nightmares. More markings, scratches and bruises showed up daily. Deep depression set in me like a thick liquid I couldn't get out of. I cried daily. When I wasn't crying, I was so emotionally charged that I would yell and scream at John and the kids. I was angry and sad at the same time for no apparent reason. It felt like we had no help and there was no end from this torment in sight.

Isaiah 41:10 (AMPC)

10 Fear not [there is nothing to fear], for I am with you; do not look around you in terror and be dismayed, for I am your God. I will strengthen and harden you to difficulties, yes, I will help you; yes, I will hold you up and retain you with My [victorious] right hand of rightness and justice.

Nightmares and Visions

My dreams started changing after that month of moths. I would have terrible dreams of world cataclysmic events. I would see mass shootings, volcano eruptions, earthquakes completely leveling massive cities, and people committing unspeakable crimes against others in the streets across the globe. These apocalyptic dreams started out as if I was watching the news reel. It was as if they were the top stories and they were just getting worse and worse. I was living in such a state of fear and panic all the time that the world was about to end. Anxiety covered me along with the deep depression. I felt hopeless as I watched these nightly dreams of people hurting and dying and being told in my dream that there was absolutely nothing, I could do about any of it.

I started having other dreams as well. These were not the same as the nightmares. I would dream of beautiful places and events. Instead of being scared I was in awe of the beautiful detail and bright colors. Often, I would dream of the ranches with lush greenery and tall full trees. I would see many different types of animals on the ranch that lived and thrived alongside us and our livestock. Fields of grain in open cleared spaces would flow like honey in the wind. The air smelled sweet and birds sang from high in the trees. These dreams would bring me some peace, but they were short lived and so sporadic that I couldn't see their purpose at the time.

When I started having visons during the day, I honestly thought I was losing my mind. I would ask John if he thought I was crazy. These visions would happen at the oddest times. If I were in a large crowd of people was the worst. One day I was shopping through a super center and there were a bunch of people there. One man bumped into me and it was like I watched a movie reel of his life flash before me. Then, someone else would walk by and the same thing would happen. I would see key events that they had encountered during their life, and then I would see future events of them. None of these visons were good. I saw terrible things they had done and horrible things that would happen to them in the coming days. I left my cart inside the store, in the middle of the isle and ran out to my car. I sat there crying uncontrollably for several minutes. My eyes physically felt like they were bulging out of my head. The immense pressure in my head and eyes was almost as overwhelming as what I had seen. Although I knew these visions were not the truth, witnessing them took a mental toll on me like no other. I felt as though I had seen a thousand versions of what had happened to my friend Angi in that dream all those years ago, only to multiple people and on an even greater scale.

As I drove home, I cried and prayed for relief. I told God that if this is what it meant to see visions and dreams then I didn't want my gift. I told God I just couldn't take it anymore and I felt like I was truly losing my mind. I didn't know what was from Him or what was not. I prayed for help for the first time through all of the horrors we had been through. I finally asked God for help.

1 John 4:1-6 (ESV)

4 Beloved, do not believe every spirit, but test the spirits to see whether they are from God, for many false prophets have gone out into the world. ² By this you know the Spirit of God: every spirit that confesses that Jesus Christ has come in the flesh is from God, ³ and every spirit that does not confess Jesus is not from God. This is the spirit of the antichrist, which you heard was coming and now is in the world already. ⁴ Little children, you are from God and have overcome them, for he who is in you is greater than he who is in the world. ⁵ They are from the world; therefore, they speak from the world, and the world listens to them. ⁶ We are from God. Whoever knows God listens to us; whoever is not from God does not listen to us. By this we know the Spirit of truth and the spirit of error.

PART II: HOPE DEFERRED

61 *Kerrie M. Baker*

Proverbs 13:12 (NKJV)

¹² Hope deferred makes the heart sick,
But when the desire comes, it is a tree of life.

Speaking Out

Even with everything we were going through at home, we still had our lives to live. We had children to raise and a ranch to keep and a business to operate. We couldn't just shut down the rest of our lives, although we really wanted to. So, with a brave face we pushed on. I would go to the shop every day and smile and act like everything was fine. I had a couple of employees that seemed to catch some of the fall out of my emotional reactions to the simplest of things. They had no idea what was happening at home and I didn't feel comfortable telling them after what our own preacher had said. Besides I had this feeling that whomever I told would end up having the same problems we were. I didn't want to transfer any of my hell to anyone else. For a long time, we just dwelt with it in silence.

One day I finally spoke up to a friend. Jeanie was the secretary for the man I rented the building my shop was in. Her office was next door and we had kindled a friendship. She was funny, creative, outgoing and kind. I remember the day I told her. She came over during lunch to visit and see what new soaps and lotions I was putting out. I was crying when she walked in, and immediately she said "okay, that's it. What's going on with you?" I told her that there were weird things happening at my house and I had not gotten much sleep the night before. I only gave her vague details, but for Jeanie that was enough. With a wave of her hand and snap of her fingers she stood up and said "Oh hell no. We ain't havin' that! Come here we gonna pray and stop this right now!" She was stern in her words and movements. She took my hands and prayed against evil and works of the enemy in Jesus' name. She prayed using scriptures specific to what I had told her. I had never heard anyone pray with so much conviction and belief. She told me she knew I was going to have a great night sleep that night and that I needed to start reading bible verses that dealt with the things I was going through. Then she ran over to her office and back. Jeanie handed me a large book of scripture references categorized by type.

I did sleep better that night than I had in years. I don't think I even dreamt. I slept for nearly eleven hours and so did John. We finally had some true peace. Over the next few days, I asked her questions that she answered and showed me how to use the book to find them myself. Jeanie taught me so many things about faith and true conviction in those few days. More than anything she taught me how to be bold about Jesus. She helped form the foundation of my faith. I am forever grateful for my friend Jeanie. Her boldness and unwavering faith in Jesus pushed me out of the boat. I finally had hope that there would be an end to all the trials.

Matthew 18:20 (KJV)

[20] *For where two or three are gathered together in my name, there am I in the midst of them.*

Finding Faith

Jeanie had helped me find the door to my new relationship to God, but it took a more life changing event to make me walk through it. When the activity started up again in just a couple of weeks, I was embarrassed to tell Jeanie about it. She would ask if things were better and I would just say yes or everything is fine. I felt like I had failed the faith of my friend. I was trying, but I just didn't know how to pray like she did. I didn't know what I was doing. I would look up scriptures and read them out loud, but that didn't help. I would play Christian music all day and even as I was going to sleep, but again there was no difference. The attacks seemed to be fewer but they were not completely gone.

I traveled with my mother in law, Kay to more prophetic conferences. We purchased CDs and books with more teachings. We would listen to them as we drove, and discuss what we had heard and read. Kay taught me how to dive into and love the Word like never before. I devoured the teachings and asked her so many questions on what things meant. Most of them had historical significance. I learned more about the times the bible was written and what the people in it were going through at the time. Things really started to make more sense. The more I read about what these men and women had written about God's Word the more I strove to read it myself. I found however, that as I would try to read it, I was lost. There was no comprehending what I was reading on my own. After the experience we had at the previous church I didn't feel comfortable going to bible study and asking questions. They did not have the answers to the questions I had anyway. Searching for answers on the internet is not always a good idea when you don't have a firm foundation. You can easily get lost down a rabbit hole of bad information.

Out of the blue, I met Pastors JC and Susan Cantu when they visited my shop for the first time. I had actually met them prior at a friend's house when they were having a barbeque. That meeting was a simple hello and small talk. I don't think I even really paid much attention to that encounter at the time. There were quite a few people there and I spoke to many different ones that day. So, when they came into my storefront it was like meeting them all over again for the first time. They were shopping around, and I was visiting with my mother in law who had come down. After she left, they purchased a couple of items and then started asking me questions about Kay. At first it was as if JC had more, he wanted to say but was hesitant. Finally, he asked if I knew the woman who had just left, and if so, how well did I know her. He told me he needed to talk to her and that it was very important. When I informed him that she was my mother in law he told me very plainly that God had shown him that she had many holes in her bones and was in a lot of pain. I was floored. I didn't understand how he could know that. She was literally in the store less than five minutes while he was there. They didn't speak to each other, and he didn't know who she was or who I was. There was no explanation of how this man knew she had literal holes in her bones from years of being affected by rheumatoid arthritis. He then told me that they were local pastors at a new church in town and introduced themselves to me. I instinctively invited them over to dinner so we could visit some more, and he could talk with Kay.

Hebrews 13:17 (AMPC)

17 Obey your spiritual leaders and submit to them [continually recognizing their authority over you], for they are constantly keeping watch over your souls and guarding your spiritual welfare, as men who will have to render an account [of their trust]. [Do your part to] let them do this with gladness and not with sighing and groaning, for that would not be profitable to you [either].

Slow Start

When Pastors JC and Susan came out to the ranch it was truly an amazing encounter. He confirmed many things to us. His words of knowledge of very specific questions Kay, John & I had been having for a long time was on point. JC explained how he knew what we were asking God in our prayers, because God had told him to come talk to us. Years of grief and sorrow were healed during those few hours of conversation. They came to just give us hope and love. A new relationship was being formed that was healing to our souls.

There were still crazy circumstances and all the attacks going on, but we did not even talk about any of that. The focus was on healing deep old wounds from the past, and loving us in our grief. I knew unlike any other people I had met before, that these two understood me. I could understand them too. Pastor JC could see things others couldn't, and he gave me hope that the encounters of my prophetic gift were truly from God.

A few times after that dinner I would see Pastor JC and Susan at the shop. They would stop by to visit and check on how we were doing. I opened up to JC about dreams and visions I had been having. He would explain in great detail the meanings of them and why I was seeing what I was seeing. He began counseling and training me without me even realizing it at the time. I was still unsure and weary about fully committing to church again. Although they had offered for us to come check out services, I was not ready to take that leap. I wasn't ready to jump into attending anywhere. We live so far from town, and the kids are always so busy. I came up with multiple excuses instead of just being honest. I was scared of church. I was afraid of getting involved with people who were just going to be out to get what they could get from us. I was hesitant of being around so many new people because I was just starting to really make friends in our town. I was worried that if I went to church with a group of people and was involved in fellowship with them, they would see me and want to run. I had believed the lie that I didn't need to be around other people. I believed that I had way too much on my plate and that Sunday's were supposed to be my day to just rest from the week. I really thought I could hide from God.

I believed all of that for a couple of years. I had attended a couple of services, by myself. John was more hesitant than I was and didn't want to go with me. I was quick to go in and even quicker to leave. There were not many members of the congregation at the time, but everyone was welcoming and nice. I remained guarded and not ready to really open up. I was still trying to figure out everything. Trying to comprehend how this new church fit into my old ways of believing in God. I had tons of questions, but never wanted to ask. So, I held back and didn't want to commit to church, to God, to new Pastors. Then God used a life changing event to shake me out of my personal pity slumber.

Jeremiah 3:15 (NLT)

15 And I will give you shepherds after my own heart,
who will guide you with knowledge and understanding.

Breaking Point

My life changed in an instant. It was the day after July fourth. John, the kids and I were having a celebration for the holiday weekend. Our oldest son had just graduated in May, and a couple of his classmates had come over to pop fireworks with us on the ranch. Fireworks were always a big deal for us. We would buy lots of mortars and fountains and m eighties or black cats. We would have roman candle duels and throw black cats at each other. Sparklers would fly around in the air drawing pictures and names. We usually had to break up our firework display over two days because there were just too many to pop in a day. So, there we were in all of our Fourth of July celebration shenanigans. Popping fireworks in pajamas and flip flop shoes.

Now, I have had an issue ever since I first got sick that has never gone away. The medical term is called catalepsy. Basically, when I laugh hard or if I get scared, I lose muscle control. If you have ever heard of a fainting goat or scare goat, that is what happens to me. For years my family has thought it hilarious to startle me for this very reason. I get startled, lose control of my legs and fall straight to the floor in a heap. I cannot move for thirty to sixty seconds, but I can hear and see everything going on around me. Due to the reaction of the scare goat similarities, my family has lovingly deemed it "fainting goat". For a long time, I have had this experience but have never once been injured because of it. Except once.

On that night we were popping firecrackers and laughing and cutting up big time. As we were heading back into the house the kids and I were all joking around like we were going to toss fireworks to see if it made me faint goat. I started play running and laughing pretty hard. Suddenly I could feel my legs start to give way from underneath me. Then my laughs turned into shock as I heard a snap and fell to the ground hard. It sounded like someone had snapped a two by four. I couldn't move. It was dark, and I was in immense pain. Instantly I was sick and vomiting. I yelled to John who was about fifty yards behind me that I had just broken my leg. He honestly thought I had just fallen and was being dramatic, until he saw my son and his friends running over to where I lay on the ground. They all yelled "Dad, she's not kidding! Hurry she's really hurt!" I was twisted over at the waist to my side and my legs were straight out in front of me. There was a burning and tearing pain in my calf and ankle. My whole body started shaking. John and I both being retired paramedics knew the severity of what had happened. John sprang into full medic mode.

Shouting orders to the kids to get a chair from the dining room, pull the car around to where I was and get his wallet and cell phone, he gave them all their pecking orders. My sons picked me up off the ground and set me into a chair until they could move me into the car. I was begging John to call 911 and get an ambulance, but we lived so far that by the time they could get to us we would already be at the emergency room. So, he drove as fast as he safely could, calling the emergency room so they would be ready when we got there; with me bouncing in the passenger seat with my leg completely distorted.

My leg didn't look broken, but I had a constant feeling that the bone was actually sticking out of my leg. John thought that I may have a torn ligament and maybe that was why I felt that, but he assured me that the skin was completely intact. When I finally got enough nerve to look for myself, I could see he was right. Although my calf and shin area were very swollen, there was nothing protruding from the skin. My ankle looked horrible though. It looked severely dislocated. My left foot was facing outward to the outside so bad I could literally see the bottom of my foot without turning it. It was so badly disfigured that the x-ray technician was unable to get a clear picture. My shaking from pain had increased enough that my blood pressure was rising like crazy. I asked John to call Pastor JC to pray for me. He showed up at the emergency room just a few moments later and held my and John's hand while he prayed and gave us comfort.

Unfortunately, our local hospital is not equipped for emergency surgery, so they called an ambulance to transfer me an hour and a half away to the nearest trauma center. The trip was painful, but the paramedics were wonderful and even held my hand as I could not hold back tears. In the trauma center emergency room, they reset my ankle. Although I was heavily medicated, I screamed apparently loud enough you could hear it through the entire floor of the hospital, before passing out. After multiple x-rays and nerve tests I was sent to the operating room.

A night of fun and games and full of laughter turned into pain and tears. Once out of surgery I found out that I had severely injured my leg. The doctors could not understand how it happened by the mechanics of my fall. It was just not possible for that to have occurred. Both the bones in my leg were broken mid-calf. The outermost bone was shattered in numerous pieces. There was not enough bone left to set. They had to put in a metal rod with twelve screws to hold the more than twenty-six pieces of broken bone together. As if that wasn't enough my ankle itself was broken. The bones were completely separated from my leg. All of the tendons, ligaments and even vascular system were torn in two. The only thing that kept my foot attached to my body was skin. After a six-hour surgery everything was finally in place.

Although the surgery had gone perfectly, I was not out of the woods. I overheard the doctor talking to John and Kay telling them that he did not know if I would be able to keep my foot or even my leg. The damage I had sustained was that bad and only time would tell. For three months I could not put any weight on that leg. Then for another three months I could only put some weight on it. After nine months I was able to walk in a boot. Like a caged lion anger, depression and fear ran rampant throughout my mind.

Kay moved in with us to help take care of the kids and I while John worked feverishly on the ranches and keeping everyone going. I spent months on high doses of pain medications and unable to do much but sit. I wallowed in my own self-pity. I hated the situation, I hated the pain, I felt trapped. Crazy things were still going on in the house. Most nights I was awake because of the pain medications and when I did sleep, I was tormented worse than before. The constant attacks on my mind fueled my depressive selfish rage. Then, out of nowhere it boiled over. I was horrible to my mother in law. I screamed and yelled in her face while shaking and sweating profusely. I waved my fist in her face and cussed at her. It was like my mind had been completely taken over and I had no sense of control. My children witnessed this horror. Their mother had gone crazy town on their grandmother. The one person who was there the entire time. Regardless of how bad she hurt because of her rheumatoid arthritis; she was there. She cared for John, our four kids, and the two other kids that were living with us at the time. Kay cooked all the meals, cleaned the entire house, washed all our clothes, fixed me special snacks and goodies throughout the day. She even mailed me cards of encouragement. In an instant I made her feel like she was the worst person on the planet, because I allowed myself to be taken over by a hateful spirit in my mind.

Thankfully she didn't leave that night. Over time I was able to make amends for my actions, but it took a long time to rebuild the relationship with her. To recover the trust and friendship that I had destroyed in a few moments. I have asked and she has given forgiveness, but it will always be one of my biggest regrets. Within a month of my outburst, Kay's brother was in Kansas City when he fell very ill and became unconscious. He was in a coma and not expected to recover. Kay drove all the way from south west Texas to Missouri to be by his side. Shortly thereafter he passed away. Within a year, his wife Esther suffered a massive stroke. She was never able to recover and died as well.

Colossians 3:13 (NLT)

13 Make allowance for each other's faults, and forgive anyone who offends you. Remember, the Lord forgave you, so you must forgive others.

Chapter Four: Prayer House

Matthew 7:7 (NKJV)

7 "Ask, and it will be given to you; seek, and you will find; knock, and it will be opened to you.

Shortly after this horrific day, I saw Pastor Susan. She invited me to a gathering of women called "prayer house." Susan told me that ladies would come together to pray over numerous things and that we would share and have a meal together. She encouraged me to come and just see what it was all about. Feeling very shameful for what I had done days prior, I told her I would do my best to make it. I was still unable to drive myself, and I was too afraid to ask anyone to do anything more for me than they were already doing. So, I didn't go for a couple more months.

I did call Pastor JC however, and told him what had happened. He didn't judge me or belittle me. He didn't make excuses for me either, but he guided me in how to fix what I had done. How to make things right between me and God and between me and my family. Most of all, JC taught me how to be okay when I wasn't okay. He taught me how to really seek God the Father instead of relying on my own understanding.

By the time I finally made it to prayer house I was completely undone. My body had healed from the trauma of that summer, but my heart hadn't. Every week it seemed the ladies would pray for one another and for their families with great conviction and grace. All I could do was cry. The more

I attended prayer house the more and more I read my bible and asked God to make it clear to me. The more I read and asked, the more He delivered. I began understanding His Word like never before.

I witnessed miracles at prayer house. Healings from physical ailments, and mental illness. Healings from addiction and heartache. I saw women loving on one another like never before. They came together and believed in God like no one I had ever met. I became bolder to voice collective prayers out loud with them but that defiantly took me some time.

The first time Susan asked me to pray, I was completely lost. I told her I couldn't do it. I didn't know how to pray, and I didn't know what to say. I had no idea how to really speak to God. She told me some of the best prayer advice I have ever received. She said, "just start by having a conversation. Talk to God as if you were talking to a friend, that's it. You don't have to be fancy. Just speak from the heart."

It seemed so silly that I felt like I had no idea how to pray out loud, but I always had just thought about praying. So, with my new instructions I began practicing. I would walk around the park with my cell phone up to my ear talking to God. This simple act made it easier for me to connect the open line of communication. It worked. I was praying by just talking as if talking to a friend. I told God everything about my day, what the kids were doing, how John was. Everything you would tell a best friend in normal conversation. In a short amount of time my faith was boosted to another level.

God wasn't just my creator and supreme being that was far away. He was closer to me than ever before. It wasn't long before I didn't need the phone to help me. I became bolder and spoke with more confidence to my Heavenly Father. It was as if the Holy Spirit would just tell me what to say and how to say it. My personal prayers were not just me asking God to do something for me or my loved ones. It was more about sharing every aspect of my life with my best friend. Open, honest and raw, I poured out my heart more and more, and God poured back into me.

When I would go to prayer house and pray God's word out loud for specific needs and petitions, I wasn't nervous anymore. It was like introducing a new friend to my Heavenly Father and helping them talk with Him. I never doubted if God would come through, because I just knew He would. God had given me a promise through His word that He would do it; I only needed to ask. Led by the powerful anointing of Pastor Susan, I watched as every woman there started having a different prayer language. We all spoke with boldness to our God, and saw many miracles unfold before us. Prayer truly changes everything. It is the fundamental in your relationship with God. It's not about saying words in a perfect manner or sequence, but rather just being open and coming with the character God put in you. Prayer house taught me how to talk to God, and how to wait and listen for His response.

Philippians 4:6-7 (NLT)

⁶ Don't worry about anything; instead, pray about everything. Tell God what you need, and thank him for all he has done. ⁷ Then you will experience God's peace, which exceeds anything we can understand. His peace will guard your hearts and minds as you live in Christ Jesus.

Moving Forward

My leg was healing, my faith was growing, and I felt closer to God than ever before. Though, things were better, I was still fighting demonic attacks at home. The more I dove into deeper prayer, attending church, walking out my faith, and reading God's word, the more I had to push myself to fight against the attacks.

Somehow, I had gotten the idea in my head that if I was serving God that I would not have any more problems or attacks. I assumed that it would just all go away. That was just not the truth. In fact, things got even more intense. It was like living in a battle ground in the middle of a fight between good and evil. I would strive every day to read, listen, pray and learn. To have my nights filled with fear, anxiety, sickness and depression. The nightmares increased in severity. The strange occurrences at the house increased as well. More than all that, my health decreased. I was left feeling overwhelmed and as if I wasn't being a good enough Christian.

Through all of it God used me to give words of encouragement to others. He led me to pray for people and love on people. God used me to speak to strangers and new friends to give them comfort and many times confirmation of what He had already been telling them. So, I pressed in more and more. I spoke with my pastors more and more for guidance and strength, and I finally told them about everything that had happened.

Even though I was afraid they would give me the same response I had received before, I told them. Well-seasoned in these types of happenings they sprang into action. For the next few weeks, they taught John and I about taking authority in Jesus name. They also taught us about acts of faith and how to keep moving forward. More than anything, they taught us about relationship with the Father instead of religion. Through prayer, reading God's word and fasting our mindsets began to change. We cleaned the house and land with authority. We took control over our entire situation in Jesus name. We weren't and still are not perfect, but we learned how to equip ourselves better for the fight. Little did we know how much we were going to need it all.

Luke 10:19 (NLT)

19 Look, I have given you authority over all the power of the enemy, and you can walk among snakes and scorpions and crush them. Nothing will injure you.

The Shop

While trying to get back on my feet from breaking my leg I had miss managed my business. My once thriving little shop wasn't doing as well. Although business itself was diminishing, the relationships with people in town started to flourish. It was during this time I hired a lady by the name of Cacy. She came into the store and told me that she was from our small town and had just moved back. Cacy was looking for a job and was hoping I had an opening. Although I knew I couldn't provide many hours or high pay, I knew I had to hire her.

From the first moment I had met her God gave me some great insight into His plans for Cacy. Standing in the middle of the store, the Lord gave me a word of confirmation for her. I told her, "girl, I have to tell you something, and I am not quite sure how you are going to receive this, but I have a message for you." Cacy kind of giggled and timidly said okay. So, I proceeded to tell this woman, whom I had never met before that God had given her a mighty gift, her voice, but it was not in the way she was thinking. It has more to do with the people you will be able to reach and give hope to. Your voice is more than your talent, and God is wanting you to start walking in what He put in your heart to do from a young age.

She stood there, wide eyed, looking at me and back to my other employee, and then back to me. She told me she was completely shocked. Mirna, my other employee at the time told Cacy, "I promise I haven't told her a thing." I was confused by her statement and had to ask what it was she had not told me.

With a humbleness she explained that she was in fact a singer. She had recorded many albums with Tejano groups, and just recently had decided to go on her own as a solo artist. Not only was she a professional singer, but she had won five Grammy awards. Cacy then went on to tell me a story from when she was a little girl.

She was about nine or so and would watch church and worship on television. She had told her mother, that someday she would be singing for the Lord just like those people she was watching. Cacy also informed me that the pull to sing Christian music had never left her, and that she always felt it was what she was supposed to do. Although, never had anyone mentioned that to her because she was a Tejano artist, and that industry had consumed her voice.

This moment was vital for Cacy Savala-Briseno. She began going to church and serving on the worship team. Her beautiful tone and honest love for the Lord grew. More than all of that, God used Cacy to speak Jesus to many people with love and grace. Many times, during a Tejano performance, Cacy was open about her relationship with God. Often, she would pray with fans before or after her set. God opened doors for her to walk into areas where people needed Him the most. She began writing and recording Christian music. Cacy went to prayer house often, and her love for prayer and God's Word abounded. There were a few times when Cacy was working on material for a Christian album while at the shop. She would tell me how much it meant to her to write new music for the Lord. God never fails to show up during those moments. Inspiration would abound and I began writing song lyrics. Almost immediately as she read them, she would begin humming a melody to match the words. During the women's conference we held that next year, Cacy sang one of those songs. Her voice reached past the rafters of the church and through the hearts of those attending.

Now she has a new band and has fully committed her life to serving God with not only her musical talents, but with her ability to speak God's word with confidence and love. God had used me to remind his beloved daughter of her childhood dream.

The next few years my storefront was a struggle. Business was not all that great, and I never seemed to fully financially recover. However, Cacy was just one of the many people that I had the opportunity to help. God guided me to tell people things, and to just love on them. Looking back on the struggle of owning my own business I realized it was never about selling items. It was simply the avenue God needed me to take in order to reach the ones He wanted reached. In many ways, the first-person God reached through that store, was me.

1 Corinthians 12:8 (NKJV)

[8] for to one is given the word of wisdom through the Spirit, to another the word of knowledge through the same Spirit,

Returning the Favor of Faith

I had been telling my mother all about prayer house and what God had been doing in my life. So, when she was able to come in for a visit and attend with me, I was super excited. Mom opened up during that evening to all the ladies whom she had never met before. She was honest and bold, and asked for prayers over her health. I was not aware until that night, that she had been having some alarming health issues. She was worried because they had run many tests at the doctor's office the day before she and my dad had driven the six-hour drive to visit. She did not know anything for sure, but she knew her body was not healthy.

Those Godly women didn't hesitate. They laid hands on her and prayed against all attacks on her health in Jesus name. They prayed with conviction over her. They loved on her as if they had known her their entire lives. No doubt God had orchestrated her being at prayer house that night.

About a week later, she called me with terrible news. Her lab results had come in and she had a fairly rare form of skin cancer. Holding back tears, she informed me that the doctors told her she would undergo chemotherapy and radiation, and that this was a type of cancer that could not be surgically removed. She also told me through her weeping raspy voice that it was stage four. Not only was it as severe as this type could be, but there was absolutely no cure for it. The doctors had told her that all the treatments were aimed at prolonging her life as best they could, but that the prognosis was not good long term. At most she had five years left.

I cried with her and my dad on the phone as she delivered the grim news. Those immediate emotions were flooding all our hearts with hopelessness and despair. I could really understand how she was feeling remembering being told similar news. It's a shock to your system to hear someone tell you that you did not have very much time left to live. With lots of "love you's" said, I hung up the phone and cried out to my Father.

Words of intercession for my mother flowed out of me. Things I didn't even know I was really saying were racing out of my heart. I told God everything and asked what I could do to help her. In that moment, the Holy Spirit reminded me of bible verses. It sprang to mind, and I grabbed my bible that I had begun carrying with me everywhere, and I looked it up. I highlighted the verses, wrote them down on a piece of paper and read them out loud. God impressed on my heart to take this to my mother and sit with her in person and teach her how to pray God's Word over her life and situation. It was a couple of days before I could get there, but I did as God had put in my heart. I told her, God wants you to pray these scriptures over yourself asking Him for more years of life and He will grant them to you. We read 2 Kings 20:1-7 together, and then she took her bible and went into the other room.

My mother endured the chemotherapy and radiation treatments for weeks, but she became severely ill from them. When she could no longer eat or even sip water, my father called my sister and I to come see her. Dad told me that he was afraid that if she couldn't eat or drink that she would die very soon, and he needed us to be there to help her get food and water down. My sister and I arrived the next day to find my mother sitting in a recliner style chair. She was frail and very thin. Her hair had started falling out from the treatments and she could not speak. There was no strength left in her hands, and she could not hold even a teacup. Dad was crying and begging her to take sips of water and pleading with her to not give up. After some coaxing we finally got her to drink a little water, and then she had enough strength to tell us the inside of her throat was severely burned from the radiation. Even small amounts of water were excruciating, and food would get stuck on the dry scaly burns. It was extremely difficult for her to talk, and she ended up writing down short phrases and yes or no so that we could have a small conversation. I sat on my knees beside her and prayed her scriptures out loud. She could not do it herself and had not been able to for at least a week. In that moment she had concluded that she was going to die.

God had another plan for her life. That afternoon I called Cancer Treatment Centers of America. God just kept putting it in my mind that I had to contact them. After a few phone calls and getting paperwork together, my father flew with my mom to Atlanta for an evaluation. Within a couple of weeks my mother became more vibrant and fuller of hope for her life. She was even able to return to work as a teacher while undergoing the new treatments from their center. After a long grueling several months, my mother rang the done with treatment bell. Not only was she deemed cancer free, the doctors had told her they now had a plan to heal others who had the same type of cancer. My mother was the first person to be cured of an uncurable cancer.

I do not know exactly how many years my mother asked God for on that first day of her prayer. I do, however, know that God is faithful. He gave those doctors ways to heal my mother as well as countless others. He has given her years of healthy life. He uses her daily to still teach children and to serve in the nursery at church. Her life has not been easy, and those years have been met with struggles, but God is faithful.

Jeremiah 30:17 (NKJV)

[17] *For I will restore health to you*
And heal you of your wounds,' says the Lord,
'Because they called you an outcast saying:
"This is Zion;
No one seeks her."'

Two Weeks Later

I will never forget the phone call I received from my mother two weeks after she was declared cancer free. She was frantic and almost crying.

"Kerrie," she said frantically, "something is wrong with your dad. I think his blood sugar is messed up, but the tester says it is normal, but I think he's really sick and I don't know what to do."

I switched into paramedic mode from daughter mode. This was a normal experience for me with my parents. Anything medical related I would get a phone call and have to answer questions from a medical perspective or help decipher medical terminology after a doctor's visit they had. This was different.

"Okay, mom," I spoke as calmly as I could, even though I felt as though I had been punched in the gut. "Tell me what is going on exactly."

She said, "Well, he was acting kind of weird, like how he does when his blood sugar gets low, so I checked it and it was like one hundred and ten, but then he started throwing up like all over the place."

"Mom!" I exclaimed with some authority due to her panic in her voice. "Where is he, and is he still throwing up?"

"Oh, no," she said, more calmly. "He is lying on the bed crying, rolling around and grabbing his head. He says it hurts so bad!"

As calmly as I could I managed to tell her, "Mom, right now, hang up and call 911. Do not call me back until the ambulance is on its way!"

With shaky hands I hung up the phone and then immediately picked it back up to dial my brother Dennis. He had been staying with mom and dad for a while, and I was unsure if he was there or not. I prayed he would be close enough to get there, since I was six hours away. In two rings he answered.

"Dennis, are you home?" I questioned him before he could even really say hello.

"Yeah, sis. What's up?" He knew my voice was serious and he matched my tone.

"Dennis, I just got off the phone with mom. Go right now and make sure she is calling 911. Dad is having a massive stroke!" I was trying not to yell.

I heard him going across the house to find our parents, while telling me he had been there and did not know why they had not just come and got him. He had no idea that anything was going on. I did my best to assure him that it was just because mom didn't know how severe the situation was, and how she thought the blood sugar monitor was messing up. He reached their bedroom, and told me that yes, she was talking to 911.

"I'm getting my things together and I am on my way. I will see you in a few hours. Please let mom know. I love you brother," I rushed to say and hung up even before he could reply.

Full panic attack hit me like a load of bricks. I was running through the house shaking and crying. Trying to pack a bag and explain to John what was happening. It was late at night and the kids were already in bed except for our oldest. He had already graduated high school and was home in between semesters. We decided that John needed to stay with the other kids and Cristopher would ride with me or help me drive since it was so late. By the time I got myself together enough to pack a bag my mother had called back and told me that the ambulance had taken dad to their local hospital and she and Dennis were waiting on the doctor. I rushed to finish packing and Cristopher and I headed out. Before we had even left the driveway, my mother had called back and told me they were flying my dad to a hospital in Ft. Worth and that he was in fact having a major stroke.

I prayed as we drove what was supposed to be a six-hour drive and called my brothers and sister. After only four and a half hours later I pulled into the parking lot of the hospital. The sun was not even close to coming up when we walked in at five thirty am. We had left the ranch at 1 am. Dad was already in the critical care unit and was being prepped for surgery. We made it to his hospital room just in time to hear the neurosurgeon speaking to my mother.

Speaking very plainly the doctor said, "Mrs. Richardson, your husband is bleeding in his brain. We are going to go in a stop the bleeding, but I do not know exactly what is causing it until we get in there. I will be honest with you; it is a miracle that you were able to get him to us in time to be able to do anything. We will do all we can to save your husband, but you need to be prepared. The next twenty-four hours will tell us more, but if he has any other family, you need to call them. I do not think he will survive for much more than that."

As the doctor turned and left the room, I saw my mom sitting there holding her phone trying to call the rest of the family. Her still frail fingers were shaking and unable to press the numbers. She looked up at me and started to say that if I hadn't made her call 911 then this would have been different. I cut her off, and explained that I did not make her, and that it was a push from the Lord to make those actions. We called everyone we could to pray for my father, and then waited for hours after they wheeled him into surgery.

By the time he was out of surgery, and back in the room, my sister had made it in from Louisiana. We stood there with my mother looking at our dad. He was hooked up to all kinds of monitors and tubing, but he was breathing on his own. He began talking to us and telling stories that made no sense before falling back asleep. The doctor arrived shortly after to tell us they had found multiple spots where he had been bleeding in his brain and that he was not out of the woods yet. The doctor said there was a lot of damage that all the blood and swelling had caused that at any moment dad could pass away.

For three days, we went back and forth between "he's going to pull through, and he has another bleed, and he's not going to make it". This yo-yo between hope and despair was brutal on all of us. My three brothers, my sister and I would go in to see dad in shifts. We all got hotel rooms near the hospital and when we couldn't be with dad, we would go back to the hotel and sit in the lounge and visit. As traumatic as it was, I was happy to spend time with all my siblings. The oldest of us I had not seen or spoken to in almost twenty years. In fact, all of us had not been together for as long as I could remember in our adult lives. We tried to be positive, but all I could see at the time were the numbers on his machines. It was the second oldest who kept us all together and reminded us that we needed to do the one thing we could do. Pray.

Dad started to become more alert. He began talking with us more and asking to see everyone he could. John and my brother in law came in to visit. The nurses began letting all of us go in together to see him, and we all laid hands on him while we prayed. We thanked God for his life, and asked God to heal him.

I was still riddled with emotion and questions. That evening, as we were all walking out after visiting hours were over, God spoke to me. He asked me if I really believed He could heal my dad. With tears welling up I said of course Lord. Then He told me He wanted me to pray. This was shortly after we had all prayed over dad. Confused, I questioned what He meant. I thought I had been praying this whole time. God told me that I was about to encounter three people before I left the hospital, and that when I met them, I would know. He then told me that when I saw them, I was to go up and ask to pray with them.

I was exhausted, mentally, physically, and emotionally exhausted. Now, after all that we had been through, God was asking me to meet three random people and ask them if I could pray for them. I remember thinking how in the world is that going to happen because we are in a big city, at a big hospital, and there are tons of people here. Just as if God heard my heart, He scolded me, and said yes, you will see three people, and you will pray with them, you are not the only one who needs help tonight, and I will show you how.

None of my family, except my parents and husband, knew about how God had used me in this way before. I did not want to put added stress on them by talking to random people in the hospital. As we got closer to the elevator, I saw a man and two women sitting on a bench in between the two elevator doors. As I approached with my family God told me that those three were the ones I needed to go talk to.

Fighting the inner turmoil between not wanting to disappoint my Lord, and my family thinking I was crazy, I looked up at my husband and told him I would meet them downstairs. There was a bathroom beside the elevator, and as the rest of my family made their way onto the elevator, I made my way to it. This gave me an opportunity to separate myself to speak with my Heavenly Father without anyone around to inhibit what I felt He was about to do.

After gaining my composure and some bravery, I walked out of that bathroom. Sure, enough the three people were sitting there, and I made my way over to them. The hallway was quiet as it was close to midnight, and there was no one else in any direction. I went up to the lady sitting on the far end to my right and asked if I could pray with them. Looking up from her cupped hands covering her face she nodded. The man and the woman with her looked at me very surprised, but they all clasped hands as I clasped her and began to pray.

I had never met these people before, I did not even ask for their names at the time. I just prayed whatever God put in my heart to say. I asked God to give them comfort as they were going through this with their sister. I thanked God for working miracles and healing their sister from the trauma she had endured in her head injury. I asked for peace for all her family to know that God was in control, and that no matter what the doctors were saying before, that God had the final word. I prayed and thanked God for her total healing and for the removal of hurt and anxiety from the rest of her loved ones. By the time I said amen and opened my eyes, all three were staring at me with their mouths hanging open and tears flowing down their cheeks. The woman sitting in the middle was shaking her head in disbelief saying there was no way I could have known any of that. I stood up, from my kneeling position and pushed the button to call the elevator. I told them that I didn't have to know because God knew, and He loved them so much. I stepped into the elevator and just before the doors closed, I noticed that the bench they were sitting on was just below the sign for the emergency room door.

On the ride down to the bottom of the hospital, I asked God to forgive me for not wanting to do His will. I prayed some more for the unknown family, and asked God to continue to bless them. God once again spoke to my heart, and said my father would be healed, and that it was all going to be okay. When I reached the ground floor, only my husband stood there waiting on me. I ran to his arms and started crying and telling him what had happened. He just held me and said he figured it was something like that.

Two weeks later, my father was released from the hospital. He had some deficit, but was able to walk and talk, and even play a little golf. Our family grew even closer after that. We all started to make more frequent trips to see mom and dad. It seemed as though all of us had grown some in our faith and we were more focused on our Father in heaven. Then just a few weeks later, it happened again.

This time I was there when it started. I sat with him on his bed as he cried holding his head until the ambulance got there. I stayed with him in the hospital as much as they would let me. He couldn't speak. He couldn't move much. The nurses would come in and try to get him to eat, but he couldn't. I finally started feeding him, although he did not like the pureed hospital food. He seemed to make some progress, but mostly he would sleep. One whole day he slept. Even when the nurses tried to get him to sit up on the side of the bed he would not wake up.

After the nurses finally listened to me and left him alone to rest, I stood by his bedside and prayed. I saw a vision of my dad. It was like looking into a cloud that was floating above his hospital bed. It was clear and vibrant. There was a large oak tree to the left shading a large lush green field. Directly in front of me was a wooden park bench. My dad was sitting there with his back to me, turned slightly to his right talking to someone. As the picture pulled back, I could see Jesus sitting facing my dad and holding his hand. They seemed to be having a wonderful conversation. Jesus told my father that he had a choice. He could come with Him now, or he could stay a while longer, and come later, but that only my dad could choose.

I leaned over to my dad, still asleep on the bed, and told him I was going to have to head home. I then told him, I loved him and whatever he chose would be okay. I promised him I would take care of mom if he wanted to go with Jesus. Then I told him, that if he wanted to come back that he was going to have to work very hard, but he could do it. I kissed him on the forehead and left the room. He never woke up or flinched.

Two weeks later, I got a phone call from my dad. His words resonated in my ear as well as my heart. He was crying as he said, "Baby girl, I just wanted to call you and let you know I am here, and I am working very hard." My mom then got on the phone and told me that he had been wanting her to call me for three days to tell me what he just had, but that he had not been able to truly speak until then.

Not long after, my parents moved in with my sister in Louisiana. The first time I went to visit them, since they were now twelve hours away, dad had another stroke. Before leaving the hospital the first night he grabbed my hand and said he had something to tell me. "Baby girl, I just want you to know I love you and I am proud of you. I am not going to be here much longer, and I need to tell you something. Listen to me this time for sure, okay? I need you to know that I do love you and I am going to have to go, but when the time comes, for you to go where I am headed, I will be the first person there to greet you with a big hug. Just so you know, the angels will sing with you one day. They will sing songs that you write. I love you."

The doctors sent him home on hospice. Within a couple of years, he was completely bed ridden, and couldn't speak. After nearly four years on hospice, my father passed away, with my mother, sister, and I singing praises and hymns to God at his bedside.

Ephesians 6:1-4 (NKJV)

1 Children, obey your parents in the Lord, for this is right. 2 "Honor your father and mother," which is the first commandment with promise: 3 "that it may be well with you and you may live long on the earth."

4 And you, fathers, do not provoke your children to wrath, but bring them up in the training and admonition of the Lord.

Ecclesiastes 3:1-8 (NKJV)

[1]*To everything there is a season,*
A time for every purpose under heaven:

[2]*A time to be born,*
And a time to die;
A time to plant,
And a time to pluck what is planted;
[3]*A time to kill,*
And a time to heal;
A time to break down,
And a time to build up;
[4]*A time to weep,*
And a time to laugh;
A time to mourn,
And a time to dance;
[5]*A time to cast away stones,*
And a time to gather stones;
A time to embrace,
And a time to refrain from embracing;
[6]*A time to gain,*
And a time to lose;
A time to keep,
And a time to throw away;
[7]*A time to tear,*
And a time to sew;
A time to keep silence,
And a time to speak;
[8]*A time to love,*
And a time to hate;
A time of war,
And a time of peace.

Chapter Five: Coming Full Circle

With everything that had happened I still was fighting my own inner battle. I had held on to fear and anxiety for so long. I had witnessed miracles, wonders, terrible events and numerous deaths. The circumference of life had been unfolding before my very eyes. Still, I had those demons beating me down.

After talking with my dad his last time in the hospital, I kept wondering if he was alluding to me not being around here much longer too. I was conflicted in my heart. I knew God had healed me, but at that time, I was just coming up on my end mark the doctors had given me. It was coming closer at an alarming rate.

As the months went by leading up to my thirty eighth birthday, I let fear grip me. I was tired and worn out. My body hurt all the time. I was outwardly walking as if I believed my healing. Inwardly, however, I felt like I was fighting a losing battle. Depression came in with fear. I couldn't move very much due to the physical effects those things had on me. I was constantly exhausted, and my body hurt so badly. The headaches increased and I could not do much but sleep.

About the week before my birthday, Pastor JC called and asked if I would be willing to share a bible teaching at the church on the next week. I dove in and studied God's word even more. I prayed hard about what to say. When the time came for me to deliver the word God had given me, all I could do was praise Him. Honestly focusing my attention on God, made all the rest of my physical, emotional and mental issues fade.

I beat the odds. I overcame ten years' worth of hell. On my birthday I stepped out in faith and taught the word of God to my local peers. What an amazing honor. Overcome with emotion, I began crying in front of the congregation. I was so happy and humbled at the same time. God spoke to my heart right there. I began telling some of my testimony as I taught His word. My teaching and preaching were far from perfect. I stumbled over my words, messed up explaining some things and had to back track to my notes. I could only speak for about half the time that I was supposed to teach, when God pushed me to just pray. Although I felt as if I had failed in bringing the perfect message to the people, God used all my shortcomings to give others confidence to be bold and step out on his faith. Completely in spite of me, my friends sitting there could see what God wanted to show them.

That night, before I fell asleep, I prayed with tears flowing down my cheeks. I thanked God for everything. I could hear Him speak right back to me. With sweet love and total understanding God told me this was just the beginning. He never promised it would be easy. He never said He would make my life perfect. He just reminded me that he was always with me, just as my father had told me all those years ago.

Since that day, God has proven Himself to me time and time again. He has used me to love on people. God has pushed me out of my comfort zone into His glory. He has taught me how to really walk out His word. He is not just God. He is my God.

Psalm 46:1-3 (NKJV)

[1] God is our refuge and strength,
A very present help in trouble.
[2] Therefore we will not fear,
Even though the earth be removed,
And though the mountains be carried into the midst of the sea;
[3] Though its waters roar and be troubled,
Though the mountains shake with its swelling. Selah

Epilogue/Conclusion

Over the course of ten years, I went from meandering through life to living through faith. God touched my heart and changed my perspective in so many ways. He gave me giftings and taught me how to use them. He gave me a voice and showed me when to speak. Yes, it was hard. Yes, it was bone chilling scary at times. Yes, it was heartbreaking too. Yes, it was absolutely worth it to say yes to Jesus.

There are some hard lessons that I have learned through all of this. Your calling is going to crush you. If you are called to heal the sick, then be prepared to go through illness. If you are called to help the brokenhearted, then be prepared to have some personal heartache. If you are called to empower people, then be prepared to have your self-esteem attacked. Yes, if you are called, your journey will be met with hardships. These are not to hurt you or keep you from your destiny. They are to push you into where God wants you to be. If you understand the problems others face, then you are more willing and able to help them through them. Those hardships make your mantle authentic, humble and powerful. Your crushing will not be easy because what you will face with others won't be either. Your oil is not cheap. It comes at a great price. To whom much is given, much is expected. If you can only see and understand that ultimately, it's not about you; you will find the joy in every experience. It is always about Him.

There are many other stories that I could tell you about those ten years. Numerous other times of fear, pain, glory, strife, family and reconciliation. They only make up part of the story. Life lived intentionally, unconventional, outside of societies box and completely, unapologetically human. I follow my God on this side of normal.

Philippians 3:8 (NKJV)

[8] Yet indeed I also count all things loss for the excellence of the knowledge of Christ Jesus my Lord, for whom I have suffered the loss of all things, and count them as rubbish, that I may gain Christ

Acknowledgments

I would like to thank my family for everything.

My husband John, for always believing in me even when I didn't believe in myself, and for loving me for the un normal way that I am. John, your endless support for my late nights, and sleeping in. You are my greatest supporter and armor bearer. Thank you for praying for me and keeping me on my toes.

For my children, thank you all for keeping me young in spirit and bringing endless joy.

I would like to thank Cristopher, my oldest, for all your love and gentle spirit. You are always there for a big hug just when I need it.

To Zack, thank you for all the laughs and keeping me grounded to be my weird mom self. You always find a way to keep me from getting too serious.

To Dacie, my daughter, thank you for pushing me to tell my story, and for following Christ direction in your own life. You push me to know Jesus more and more every day.

To Justin, my youngest, thank you for being my anchor, and showing me peace under immense pressure. You have taught me more than you will ever know.

To my mother, Melody, thank you for always believing in, and for never giving up on me. You are always my biggest cheerleader.

To my mother in love, Kay, thank you for being my friend and not leaving when you had every right to. Your unwavering faith in God has brought me through many trials.

For my dear friend Angi, thanks for letting me tell part of our story, and for being my timeless friend. You help me to see God in ways I could never have before.

I would like to give special thanks to my home church. New Beginnings Ozona, all of you who heard some of my very first teachings, thank you for sticking it out with me. Most of all thank you for all your prayers and love. As well as my Pastors, JC and Susan Cantu. Thank you for always speaking life into my heart, and love into my spirit. Thank you for all your teachings and pushing me to step out of the comfort zone.

John 15:12-17 (NKJV)

12 This is My commandment, that you love one another as I have loved you. 13 Greater love has no one than this, than to lay down one's life for his friends. 14 You are My friends if you do whatever I command you. 15 No longer do I call you servants, for a servant does not know what his master is doing; but I have called you friends, for all things that I heard from My Father I have made known to you. 16 You did not choose Me, but I chose you and appointed you that you should go and bear fruit, and that your fruit should remain, that whatever you ask the Father in My name He may give you. [17] These things I command you, that you love one another.

John 3:16 (KJV)

[16] For God so loved the world, that he gave his only begotten Son, that whosoever believeth in him should not perish, but have everlasting life.

Don't wait another second. God's love is pure and life changing. He wants a relationship with you. He is a good Father and desires to hear from you. Maybe you have known about Him, but do not know him as your God. It's easy to start. You simply have to believe Jesus is the Son of God, and that he paid the greatest price for you. The bible says that none may go to the Father except through Jesus. I want to encourage you to get to know Jesus. You can start today. Right here. Pray this prayer out loud. (Your voice has power!)

Lord,

I have heard of your love. I have heard of Jesus dying on the cross for my sins, and that he resurrected on the third day. I believe Jesus is your son, God. I want to have a relationship with you. Come into my heart today Jesus; I accept you as my Lord and Savior.

Amen.

About the Author

Kerrie lives on the family ranch with her husband John and their sons Zackary and Justin. Her other two children Cristopher and Dacie share an apartment in a nearby city where they are close enough to visit often.

Kerrie loves all the animals on the ranch but enjoys having pets as well. With two healer mix dogs and one north American timber wolf hybrid, Kerrie stays well entertained. She is a stay at home ranch wife who loves to garden, paint, cook, but most of all serve the Lord.

Although painting began as a hobby for Kerrie, it has turned into a nice business. She sings praise and worship during painting sessions. When someone specifically request a painting, Kerrie prays for that person throughout the entire process, as well as reading God's word that the Holy Spirit leads her to while painting. Each buyer receives a handwritten prayer specific to them along with the artwork.

Following her love for the Lord, family is important to Kerrie. Her mother, mother in love, and one of her brothers all live close by. Most weekends are spent with family playing cards, board games, and spending quality time. Fun and laughter resonate in her home, and there is always a bit of childlike goofiness that comes along with these family game nights.

Kerrie has inspired many with her Facebook videos called Encouragements. Teaching others the love and grace of God while walking through the modern world is one her biggest passions. Kerrie serves at her local church as an in-house minister, and alongside her husband as deacon and media ministry. She lives a full life and walked through many fires by her faith in God.

Bringing God's word to life to lift other up if her true passion. The Lord has been taking Kerrie out of her home church to bring the messages God inspires to others. She speaks with passion of honesty, with unwavering dedication to the Lord. Kerrie is humble and will be the first to tell you that everything is for and from God.

Currently Kerrie is writing another book titled *The Other Side of Normal*, due to be release next year. She says that it will include more about the revelation of God's word, and more testimonies of how He uses her to help others.

Psalm 40

¹ I put all my hope in the LORD. He leaned down to me; he listened to my cry for help.

Made in the USA
Coppell, TX
15 November 2021

65796610R00066